Not Superdad

Not Superdad

How A New Dad Connected to Fatherhood Without Any Super Powers

Keith Devin Morton

Malecare, Inc. www.malecare.org
2012

Dedication

This book is dedicated with lots of love and appreciation to my son Devin, and wife Shalawn (for obvious reasons!).

Acknowledgements

I want to say thank you to my collaborator and friend Darryl Mitteldorf because without him I'm not sure I'd be helping fathers and families. Thank you to my editors, Marielle Messing and Shalawn who believed in this project and helped keep it fresh even though it's been in the making for approximately forever. I'd also like to thank my friends. The two who have been with me and believed in me since the seventh grade (Kirt and Tasha, of course!). And the newer ones who have been loyal and supportive through thick and thin—and who through it all have not given up on me and fired me. To all the family (especially Ma and Uncle Craig) who ever showed love and helped keep me out of trouble when I was living at "402." Peace to my brothers who will always hold a special place in my heart because they never doubt me even when I doubt myself. We share a bond that is sealed by the shared blood that flows in our veins and a true faith in one another. A special thank you goes to Mama Mattie who throughout these stories was often in the background babysitting and playing with her great-grandson along with Aunt Jeanette. Nana Cynthia, you are the best! Mom and Dad thank you for life. And to all the dads and moms and bloggers who have appreciated what I have been trying to accomplish over the years.

Cheers!

READING THIS BOOK

This book is a snap shot of a two year period in my life that I could never have predicted. I've been writing this book in some form since my boy was born. Some of it was written during my last six months of college, which just happen to correspond with the early months of my son's life. My boy, Devin, was born in the midst of projects and term papers, when finals were just around the corner.

The book opens with several pages of sweetness highlighting the birth of my boy and all of the emotions that come along with such a powerful event. Quickly after that tale is told, we jump into a chronicle of my being a father through my son's terrible twos *and* threes—it was a heck of a time. As of this writing, my son is four years old and I'm relieved to say that we are officially out of that phase. Devin has become one of the smartest, funniest, friendliest, and most loving and thoughtful people I know. Part of his growth is just that—getting older.

Another component is dedicated and attentive parenting. We finish off with advice and tips for fathers of young kids. Being a new Dad is one thing, raising an African American child to be the best that they can be is another. You and I are going to get through this thing, and, I think this book will help. It's got lots of talk I wish I had heard when my son was born. I made the book a short read because I want you to quickly take away from it what you need, and then get back to being the best dad that you can possibly be!

Let's start.

Prologue: The Rise of the New Dad

I'm a New Dad, I'm also black. And I'm one half of the team that is raising a black boy. This has its own unique challenges: My son is statistically more likely to drop out of school, go to prison, end up unemployed, and be murdered. These harsh realities add a layer of urgency to parenting that few can comprehend without the first-hand experience of being the father or mother of a black boy. Through my online escapades I have found not only black folk that understand the sheer weight of this challenge, but also several white people who have adopted black children. What I find in these instances is that though we do not share a common ancestry, we do share the awareness associated with raising kids that are not expected to flourish in this society.

Ever since I became a father, I've come across the term "Superdad" just about everywhere I turn to for parenting advice for fathers. It's on the Internet. It's on the dust jackets of books. It's been used in online parenting magazines, and by major mainstream print magazines like *Time*. I've even heard the term on radio and television, and it's all over the blogosphere. The word "Superdad" reeks in our daily parenting lexicon.

And yet, I have never met a single Superdad. I've met plenty of really great and attentive dads, just none with superhuman abilities. Next time you see a book or magazine gloating about "superdads," do the next dad a favor. Drag that sorry, inflated tome over to the fiction section.

After years (ok, a few hours) of intense research (and several bowls of Phish Food ice cream) I believe I can profile the mythological Superdad, or SD for short.

- SD presents himself as someone that can change a diaper with one hand, while preparing a bottle of formula with the other. Unsanitary, yes, but SD knows no bounds!
- SD tends to the psychic and emotional needs of his child through speaking perfect and fluent baby-ese, by cooing and goo-gooing with the diction of a trained Shakespearean actor. He does this, of course, while standing on one foot reciting the Spanish alphabet (because a Superdad's kid must know a second language, any second language, and it matters very little that the kid doesn't speak English yet).
- SD bakes cookies on Saturday and goes to Mommy and Me classes on Sunday. He sometimes brings the cookies he bakes to share with the class.
- SD is caring, understanding and flexible, to a point that many find disturbing. He has been known to cry with his child during particularly intense days of teething.
- SD is dripping love from every pore, ready and willing to do whatever it takes to see to it that his child's every need is met. He

knows his child's needs before all others, including the child. This is not a bad thing. But, it often is an impossible thing.

The schedule SD keeps is the envy of drill sergeants around the country. His co-parent is in awe of his abilities and thanks the heavens every day for him being alive. Where does he get all of his positive energy from!?

Nowhere. This dude does not exist.

However, a version of him, if you can call it that, does exist. The *other* version is somewhat flawed. Let's call him New Dad (ND). New Dad generally has good intentions and wants his child to be happy and healthy just like any ordinary father that loves his family with sincere, reckless abandon. From someplace deep inside, ND knows that raising a child is the most significant thing that he as a man can do, and is acutely aware of the thousands of ways he can muck it up. He's more complicated than SD. He gets more bullet points.

- ND jumps in to help out or to "handle it," only to discover that his intervention was either not needed, or a bit overzealous. He puts the kid in a dusty old two sizes too small diaper, not realizing that a brand new box of pull-ups was in the kitchen in an unpacked shopping bag (he was asked twice to unpack the shopping bags).
- ND is the dad that when asked by his co-parent to help the kid put on a pair of

white sneakers watches the poor kid limp away because his co-parent was referring to the *other* white sneakers. The pair that actually fits.

- ND can't find a single matching outfit in the mountain of clothes he tossed from the neat dresser drawer to the toy-strewn floor. He closes his eyes and selects an outfit, deciding that a funky look for the child will go well with his now funky mood.

- ND tries to join the games that his child plays, and is abruptly kicked out of the session with a point, a wave, and a surprisingly clear, "go away daddy," because ND doesn't know the rules. (Yes, a two year old will kick you out of a game as punishment for your ignorance.)

- ND is a bit lazy and without hesitation, will skip several dozen pages in a certain unreasonably long children's book about a cat wearing a hat.

- ND never washes his kid's hair because he thinks that the natural oils give it style, and he's all about style. (*No, he's not.*)

- His child cries and ND asks "Hey kid, why are you crying?" He doesn't know why his child is crying and refuses to pretend that he does, except when it's obviously bedtime, feeding time, or teething—then he pretends with the best of them. He may not know why his child is crying every single time, but he does care about *why* every single time.

- ND doesn't want to do anything when he gets home from work, except, maybe, sit on his sofa, watch TV, and scratch a little bit. But, he knows deep in his being that he must be a significant part of the life of his little one. What's strange about this guy is that every single time he gives up a favorite TV show to play with, bathe, or eat with his child, he is glad he did and can't understand why he thought twice about it.
- ND is also a little dumb, and will forget how much fun he had bonding with his offspring after giving up some downtime. Week after week at "Mommy and Me" class (yes, he shares this similarity with SD), he has a ball banging on the drums, ringing the bells and singing the clean-up song with the kids cheering him on. Nonetheless when Sunday comes around and it's time for class, he tries to come up with a creative excuse to get out of going.

He is a mess.

He is a tad off.

He is New Dad. The *not* Superdad.

New Dad is thrilled that he's a parent, despite the fact that he's not that amazing at it. He works hard toward improving himself personally and professionally, and prioritizes taking care of himself because he wants to live long enough to reap the benefits of decades of parenting. New Dad worries daily about the welfare of his family, but knows where his power lies and plays upon his strengths. The future is important to him because he knows that what he puts in his child's mind and heart today will shape the adult person that he will surely become.

I'm a New Dad. Sometimes I simply have what my son Devin needs at the right moment, be it a hug, a belch (belching amuses him), a toy in my pocket at the mall, or a chicken nugget. Other times I'm clueless and useless, lost in my own home and head. But it's OK. My occasional blank-page parenting is not detrimental to the development of my child. If I can't figure out how to make him eat his veggies today, tomorrow, or the next day, he will not go hungry. If I can't determine the appropriate activity for him on a Saturday, well, that's what co-parents are for. If you don't have a co-parent, get one.

I am not necessarily promoting marriage inasmuch as I am promoting co-parenting for the sake of maintaining one's sanity. Keep in mind though that co-parenting is nothing to take lightly and if done incorrectly can be much more emotionally draining than single parenting. Oh yeah, and love, or something like it, also comes in handy when parenting a child with someone else.

New Dads draw blanks. Sometimes, they can make the wrong disciplinary decisions. Not the end of the world. As long as you learn from your mistakes, and make the proper adjustments in the future, you are doing all that you can. The reality is that being a dad is a big scary job with long hours, no pay and limited vacation time. And for the most part, you are expected to suck at it because dads have been given low expectations by society. And, much of society is surprised that good black fathers even exist. So, if you do enough to not suck, you have already reached the upper echelons of being a dad.

However, mediocrity should never be a dad's goal. Sure, your child will be fine if you are the definition of mediocre (this holds the most truth if you have a great co-parent). Children are resilient and driven—it's almost innate. Their minds are like little bloodsucking leaches slurping up all of the new knowledge that they come across. They latch onto a concept until they have what they need from it and move on. Your job is to make their job of learning-through-living a fun, and healthy experience. And if you are actively involved, then they will most certainly be having more fun and their experiences will be deeper and more meaningful as a result. Remember these simple formulas:

- **static involvement = mediocrity** (example: you go to the children's museum and watch your kid wander and touch the interactive exhibits. You check your watch regularly.)
- **dynamic involvement = fathering excellence** (example: you let your child select the exhibit she wants to start with at the children's museum and explain it in a way that she understands, then you both touch and play with the interactive exhibits. Your watch is in your pocket because

you don't want it to get wet while you play with the water wheel!)

A New Dad is a flawed hero. He's the Bizarro Superdad, if you will. He is not perfect, and never will be. His goal is not perfection in being a dad, or anything else for that matter, because with all of his imperfections, he understands that seeking perfection in life is a waste of time that could have been spent having fun with the family. He's content with fulfilling his need for perfection through bowling the perfect game, or barbecuing the perfect steak, or of course, doing a perfect impression of Elmo just to see his child smile.

Being a parent, no matter your race, is a challenge. Being a dad is almost a separate challenge because many of us are fighting to undo negative social mores that have been passed down over the generations. We are fighting stereotypes and rewriting the book on what it is to be a good dad. And we're doing it together.

PART ONE: BECOMING DAD

There are few moments in a man's life when he finds perfect clarity. One of those moments is when it dawns on him that he is now a dad. No longer can he define provider as "he who makes beer runs for the crew" or, "he who satisfies his woman with his tongue." Nope. Those days become nothing more than a vaporous memory to be recalled at infrequent boy's nights out. The new dad is forced to toss out his old definition and start thinking of provider in terms of emotional and financial stability. In terms of being there, loving. His non-parent pals don't quite get what has happened to the poor guy. But he does. He's matured, or at least should have.

I am a NEW DAD

A terse announcement from the captain, reminding all the passengers that he had just turned on the "fasten seatbelt" sign, prompted panicked whispers amongst the crew.

This was my fourth trip to Key West with my fiancé Shalawn, and so far it had been the most unnerving trip to date. I was reminded of a dream (one that many of us have had in some variation or another) where a deranged knife-wielding madman is chasing me through my hometown and I am running no faster than a ninety-year-old arthritic great grandmother through three feet of whipped cream. Only this time the madman was an airplane and I was trapped in coach.

Two flight attendants were serving drinks to the people in the row ahead of us when another crew member, an attractive black woman with dark, warning eyes, emerged from first class and whispered the world's loudest whisper stating, "The captain said that we *all* really should sit down *now*." The flight attendants looked at one another, first quizzically then with understanding. Without explanation to the people they were serving, they hurriedly packed the drink cart, went to their posts, and strapped themselves into their special shoulder harnesses.

Then, as if cued by some ominous director, the plane began to shake enough to get everyone's attention. Next, it began rocking from side to side, as if two giant kids on either wing were using the plane as a seesaw. I exchanged looks with my fiancé. We tried to smile. We had been in turbulence before, but this was different. Then the plane dropped.

Five miles above the earth, the plane dropped several feet, shook, shot back up. It did this a couple of times before its last trick—a ten-foot belly flop into a sea of white clouds. The people not strapped into their seats came out of them. Those that listened to the captain now had bruises on their abdomens to prove they were wearing their seatbelts. You could hear the screams of adults mingled with those of children. You could see people lightly sobbing into their cupped palms. My fiancé and I decided not to speak. What would we say? We held hands and waited, maybe for the voice of God. Instead we got the voice of the captain.

"Now I bet that the next time someone puts on the 'fasten seatbelt' sign, you'll listen," he laughed. The entire airplane laughed too, but not with him. If the flipping and flailing inside my soon-to-be wife's womb was any indication of how Dev felt at that moment then it's safe to assume he was not amused.

We landed in Key West at about 3 p.m., an hour later than the airline told us we would. We were dying, no, *living*, for some rest and relaxation, happy that we were on solid ground and basking in the smiling sun of the southernmost city in the United States

When we arrived at our destination, a small timeshare resort, we were shown to our quarters. It was a surprisingly nice studio apartment with a private deck and direct access to one of the resort's swimming pools. Inside the studio were a small kitchen with a glass dining table, and a living room area with a real-life Murphy bed (my experience with them until then had been limited to "Scooby Doo" cartoons). The bathroom was enormous, with mirrors lining every wall. The mirrors, I thought, were sure to encourage the vanity that so many of us harbor deep (or not so deep) within our psyches—or at the very least act as the backdrop of some hot, kinky sex. The room even had cable, a luxury we cannot afford back in the big city. We turned to MTV and my fiancé decided to change into something more comfortable and befitting the tropical weather.

Pregnant with Devin, she glowed in her sleeveless denim dress, so cute that I felt like I was engaged to a life-sized stuffed toy. I almost laughed at the thought, but stifled it in consideration of her recent self-conscious streak. We can't decide what to do next. Alcohol would be a good first choice on any trip, but not this one, at least, not for my soon-to-be mommy fiancé. My soon-to-be-wife fiancé. We walked outside and tried to figure something out.

"So what do you want to do?" she asks.

"I don't know, are you hungry?"

"It's kind of early. If we eat now then we might not have anything to do later." She's right. It's around 5 p.m. We have all night.

"Let's go see where City Hall is." I hadn't meant to say that, it just came out. Her eyes lit up, so I knew that I would have to commit to my statement. I remembered looking at a map of the area earlier and navigated us west—soon realizing that we should have gone east. City Hall turned out to be just a block and a half from where we were staying, just as the hotel clerk had said. I looked at the four-story building looming in front of us. Its red brick façade and manicured lawn were quite inviting, nowhere near as menacing as it could have been given that we'd be married in that very building the next day.

"Wow, it's really close!" My fiancé exclaimed, sounding a bit too excited.

"Yeah, it is." I took her hand and made a B-line for where the people were.

On the downtown streets, the crowds were dense with tourists and locals alike. The bars filled with people, some sober, some drunk, and the restaurant hosts and hostesses beckoned people to join them for dinner. There were families, retired people, gay people, biker people all mingling together, united by the serenity of the locale, and in some cases by booze.

Hand in hand, we warded off the quizzical stares. I surveyed Duval Street in search of a couple that looked like us; the closest we got were beer guts hanging over Bermuda shorts. If only their burger filled bellies were as cute as my fiancé's pregnant figure. Despite the emotional distress from the flight, I felt at peace.

We wandered the crowded street without a destination, a plan, or a care in the entire world. I felt her long fingers entwining mine, the metal from her engagement ring pressed against my flesh. I knew she was here, that she was not going anywhere. The fear of what our future may hold was no match against the comfort of the moment. Off in the distance, we heard rock bands competing for the affections of the lingering crowds, longing for a taste of fame.

I shrank into my surroundings, enveloped by the enormity of my situation. As I yanked myself back from the depths of my thoughts and feelings, I found myself staring at a young, perky white female who suddenly overwhelmed my senses. What was it about this girl that locked me out of my own head?

"Were those her boobs hanging out?" My fiancé asked, bringing me back to myself.

"I think so," I said coolly.

Yes those were her boobs! And she had a pretty nice rack at that. Her nipples were painted blue and the rest of her breasts were just hanging out for the world to see. I saw them, and I was uncomfortable. Her boobs were the jolt that brought me back to reality. They made me see that I am not in Key West under the same circumstances that brought me here three times before. I am not here to have sex in a garden, or pool. I am not here to drink heavily in a nightclub, or a gay bar with drag queens.

I am here to be married the day after tomorrow by a county clerk at City Hall. I am here because we had to push up the date we previously planned to get married. I am here because my fiancé is six months pregnant with my first child whose legitimacy we must ensure by eloping. I am uncomfortable because that white chick's bare breasts are offensive to me and my woman— my woman, who is carrying a developing baby in her womb. Such things are now inappropriate.

She can't drink, we can't party with near naked women, and we can't even stay out too late because my fiancé needs her rest. We are about to be parents and I hadn't thought about it for one second until I saw a pair of exposed white and blue boobs. I am uneasy and I can feel a similar vibe coming from my future wife. We take a seat together on a bench near where we are staying and try to organize our thoughts and emotions as well as replenish some lost energy.

We get up from our bench, not wanting to, and pick a long route to get us back to the rental. Along the way we chat about the past visits we have made to Key

West. We are not sure when we'll be back again, with the baby or alone, but we know we will be back. It's still the most magical place on earth for us. We walk past Ernest Hemingway's old house on our way and I know why he found this island the ultimate place to write in his late years.

It's an inspiring place. It's a place where life slows to the point where nothing matters. It's a place where you can see the sun set every night and rise every morning. It's a place where lovers go to remind themselves why they are in love and where families go to enjoy each other's company away from the stressors of big cities. It's where my brothers and I were born. The place where Shalawn and I will be wed in a couple of days—in the Domestic Violence room of the county clerk's office.

We get back to where we will be staying for the next couple of nights, fold the covers of the bed over ourselves, and hold each other in our safe, secure arms. The TV is still on and we watch music videos and feel the movement of the baby beneath many layers of flesh at the same time. We drift off to some place incomparable to our waking paradise. The gentle moon kisses us both all about our faces through the open curtains. We try not to dream of being married or having Devin, but, such dreams are too sweet to resist.

Devin's Day of Birth

I woke up in a chair, sitting in a whitewashed room. My wife, Shalawn, lay across from me, semiconscious.

She looked like she had just run the New York City Marathon—twice. Behind me I could hear the ladies from the television show "The View" yapping about nothing important enough to recall, and I wondered why the television was on in the first place. I recognized the small, redheaded nurse who almost spilled her Starbucks on me in the crowded elevator that morning. Wearing her hospital-issued green scrubs, she mechanically marched past the delivery room door. I decided to venture out of the cold room to find the person that I can feel needs me somewhere off in the distance.

I had been a feeling a little sleep deprived. I had been up past 3 a.m., working on a school project. I think it was around 5:30 in the morning when my anxious wife nervously tapped me on my chest. In her calmest voice, she said, "I think my water just broke. I heard a pop. Then I felt a gush."

She heard a pop? That sounded weird to me. She wasn't microwaving popcorn, so, in my opinion, nothing should be popping inside of her. I had then asked her the most brilliantly reassuring question I could come up with: "Are you sure?"

I was a teensy bit concerned, but not scared. Well, I was filled with so many thoughts, that I don't remember how I really felt. I recalled how we had had some minor complications early in the pregnancy, bleeding and two weeks of bed rest to be exact, so I hesitated when she asked me to look to see if there was any blood on the sheets where she sat. Thankfully there wasn't. Those sheets cost almost $200. Did I really think that? There was a wet spot there. We thought it was just pee, but the reality was that pee didn't come with a pop and that's how we knew we couldn't ignore the big truth about pregnancy. No matter how prepared you are, you will not be prepared for how real things get, very, very quickly.

The water breaking wasn't the most disturbing part for us. It was the fact that it broke six weeks early and that my wife had predicted days before the exact time when it would happen. We called the hospital and got the news that the doctor that we had spent the last seven months seeing for prenatal care was not on call that morning. We spoke to her partner, Dr. O, who advised us to get to the hospital. He would be bringing my son into the world.

He's here!

So there I was, at the hospital after a delivery that I couldn't explain in words if I tried, longing to see my minutes-old son. Elated, with legs light as wings, I floated toward the open door. Shalawn smiled as I told her where I was going, looking exhausted, but very happy. I walk slow, taking deliberate steps down the sterile hallway, aware only of the quiet squeaking sound my heavy hiking boots made on the waxed floor. The beige walls guiding my path reminded me of my bathroom at home. *Note to self: REPAINT BATHROOM ASAP.*

In less than a moment I came across a small room, where I was certain I would find my son. I could feel his little presence. The room was narrow with no windows, smaller than a prison cell. All the way towards the back of the room was a dull, orange glowing light, and beneath it, my boy. There he lay on his back in the tiniest diaper I had ever seen. On his head was a little gauze cap. He seemed to be smiling. His sleep was so peaceful that my heart grew three sizes bigger, like the Grinch's after Christmas dinner. My son was alone in a hospital room, roasting under a warmer because his body temperature was too low. *Maybe because he's not used to air conditioning*, I thought. I placed my bulky pinky finger into his little white hand and he clutched it like a smoker on his last cigarette. I thought to myself, "He's cute for a newborn, but why is my son so white? "

The red headed nurse, whose name I learned was Patty, entered the room that now seemed overcrowded with two full-size people in it. My brown eyes met her green ones and she said in a comforting and professional voice, "He's fine, don't worry." I guess my eyes had betrayed my worries.

She got to work and stuck a long silver thermometer up his newborn ass. I squirmed more than he did during this procedure. In fact, he didn't seem to notice the medically-sanctioned sodomy at all. The thermometer revealed that his body temperature was still too low, so she left us alone to chat. I was glad she left him under the warmer a little longer, secretly hoping it would give him a little more color—like a tanning booth or flame-broiling a Whopper.

I welcomed him to New York City and tried to explain to him how difficult his life will be. I also promised to be there for him until the 'brothas' from the block are pouring out a little liquor for me. "Pouring out liquor" is a ritual done to mourn the recently deceased. It's like ceremonially sharing a shot with a friend by pouring to the ground (or into a sink) what he or she would have drunk had they been there. It's all very ghetto. Not surprisingly though the ritual has its roots in Africa and can be traced back at least 300 years to Benin when this was done with both libations and food to honor the spirits of our ancestors. I knew this from reading, and I knew that Devin will know this and more, from the second, forward. Man my son is here.

I tried vigorously to hold back the tears that welled up in my sleep-filled eyes—more difficult than keeping a gang of hungry police officers out of Dunkin' Donuts on free donut day. Soon Patty returned, swaddled him in four blue, white, and pink striped blankets, and placed him into one of the bassinets. She wheeled him back to his amazing grinning mother. She was glad to see us both, which surprised me, being that not too long ago, after five and a half hours of labor, she had pushed out an almost seven pound baby with no anesthesia.

At some point time must have stopped because now time finally seems to start.

PART TWO: BEING DAD

1. DO IT YOUR WAY—All good parenting doesn't look the same.

I am not a perfect father. You will never confuse me with that guy from the TV show "Full House." My fridge is filled with Budweiser and I avoid crap-filled diapers whenever possible. I'm not the most helpful father ever, but I do have the intense desire to be a good dad. Notice that you probably want to be a good dad, too. That's why you are reading this book.

I often feel like a babysitter. I find myself on the sidelines without a coach, not knowing when to jump in and do something—but when I do know something, like dressing, feeding and putting the kid to sleep, then why don't I just do it? Why are we afraid to do it our way?

Maybe it's not always easy to live up to the precedents set by the mothers of our children. When I give my son a bath—which I'll admit I do not do as often as I would like—I don't wash his hair. When I pull him out of the tub and his hair is still dry and dull, I get the *why didn't you wash his hair?* raised eyebrows from my wife. Then I feel bad that she's not happy with the way I handled my baby chore. She, being the mother, would have had the kid's hair smelling sweet like fresh lavender.

It's very hard to impress a mother.

For example, my wife will quickly and effortlessly replace the outfits I pick out for him with clothes that fit and coordinate better. Not knowing how to dress your own kid can be discouraging. In the end we always think, *hey she's the mother, she does this more often than me so she must be right.*

Maybe that's the problem.

Maybe we should be allowed to do things the crappy way because it's our way—maybe there is no right way. So, my advice to you is, **do it your way**. If you are not reprimanded, it's all good. If you are reprimanded (and by this I mean asked to do it another way), just find out what that way is and try to do it. The key word here is *try*. If you forget how your co-parent showed you to do it, or you just disagree with his or her methods, then act like you forgot. That's fine too. The reality is that if it doesn't compromise the safety or health of your child, it's OK.

So put on the purple shirt that shows your kid's navel and the orange shorts with the pumpkin on the pocket, and head for the park! You and your kid aren't hurting anybody. And to you mothers reading this, support our efforts and know when to pick your battles, especially when you know we are trying.

2. VACATIONING—It's a crapshoot with kids, just like everything else.

Having fun is an important part of any family dynamic. It can come in a variety of forms, including going on the great American vacation: the road trip. For better or worse, a road trip can give you memories that will last a lifetime.

On our first trip to the beach, my wife and I drove a rented Chrysler Town and Country—which is a decent ride for a minivan—for 12 long hours to Myrtle Beach. To make sure that we were completely overwhelmed by our first real road trip experience, we brought our son, at that time two years old, and our mothers along for the journey.

Yes fellas, you heard right, it was me, three women and a toddler! Had I known what I was getting into… well, I probably still would have done it, because I love my family—but I would've packed some anti-anxiety medications for good measure.

My son loves riding in cars, or in this case the minivan, which he referred to as "the bus." That is a big chunk of the reason that we opted for a road trip. On the road, we kept him loaded down with juice, milk, cookies, crackers and his favorite: chicken nuggets. He doesn't eat much in terms of variety, but he'll eat the beak of a chicken nugget

We all had taken more than enough time off from work to cover the planned 5-day trip, and decided to drag it out some. We checked into a hotel just of I-95 in Richmond, Virginia

That night it was impossible to put the kid to bed. We got a good deal on this huge king suite and the kid ran laps into the night. He turned lights on and off, played in the ice bucket, turned over chairs, pressed the beeping buttons on the safe, and didn't stop. We tried to put him in his crib but he flipped out and tried to throw his leg over the bar. Realizing that this wasn't safe behavior, we took him out and let him continue running amok. He was over-stimulated by his new environment and it wasn't his fault. And it was up to us to understand it. We tried to fake sleep, but he just mulled around in the dark calling out the shapes of objects he found in the dark. Circle, he said triumphantly when he came across the ice bucket top. It took him several hours to tucker out, and fall asleep in the center of our bed. When the opportunity presented itself we moved him to the crib. Once we got over trying to put him to bed while we were on the trip, and treated it like it was his vacation too, we had some fun nights with the little maniac at the hotel we found ourselves sharing in Myrtle Beach.

Where were the grannies during all of this? Just chilling. We invited them so that they would help us with the baby and maybe give us a night or two of fun. They weren't interested. They said that the kid didn't want to be with them so they weren't going to force him. What kind of crap is that? On one out of five nights we were able to roll our sleeping baby, crib and all, over to our parent's room. We then jumped in the van, drove two minutes to a famous frozen drink spot, ordered the hardest drink they serve, had them put in their novelty sports bottles, soberly drove back to the hotel, drank the frozen love potion and then…Well I'm married so there's a certain ick factor that comes with going any further. But I'll say this: It was the best night of the trip.

The trip taught me to give my kid the benefit of the doubt when possible. Go with the flow in the name of fun and relaxation, especially when vacationing, and leave your parents at home unless you have it in writing, and notarized, that they will help you with the baby. Today the kid was in bed at 8 p.m. like normal and his later schedule during the vacation is a distant memory in his little developing mind.

Your first trip with your child is a milestone that a new dad will likely never forget. The funny thing about being a new dad is that you'll never be an old one. Sure maybe in age, but if you think about it, you are a new dad at every stage, no matter how many children you have, because what worked for one doesn't always work for the others. You are a new dad when they are born and you are up helping with the late night feedings, when you are learning the words to his favorite songs, when you are learning how to put braids and bows in her hair, when you take him to his first restaurant, teach her how to ride her first bike, all the way up to homework help, first dates, driving lessons, and shooting warning shots over the heads of her boyfriend. But make sure you miss the poor kid because it just may be my son taking her to the movies and if I have anything to say about it he'll be a damn good catch.

You'll be a new dad until you die in a hundred years, so sit back and enjoy the ride. I'm trying my best to do just that.

3. THE RESTAURANT OUTING—Planning is the key to a great family meal.

The pre-baby days when you could go out to a restaurant without thinking too hard about it may be long gone, but that doesn't mean that future evenings at a sit-down restaurant are totally out of the question. The only thing is that now you have to do what most of us real guys don't mind doing: strategize.

When my son was two, my wife and I took him to his first restaurant—a real restaurant that used real silverware. We had taken the kid to the food court in the mall with some limited success, but an actual restaurant was uncharted territory.

We were seated at a booth and he was positioned at the head of the table in a high chair. The saving grace of the evening occurred as the waiter brought out a small coloring book and crayons. Restaurants are smart! He colored on the table and his chair and I didn't care— I didn't give him the crayons, so it wasn't my problem!

Once he tired of scribbling on the table, he discovered that the book had letters and numbers that kept my little Einstein preoccupied until his French fries and chicken fingers arrived.

Part of the reason that the coloring book worked to keep Devin under control was because it was early in the evening, a few hours before his regular bedtime, and he was in a good mood. We tried it a couple of days later around his bedtime in a crowded restaurant and he was so unruly that we had to take him out of the restaurant and walk him around until his food was served. I didn't let my wife do this alone because he was behaving outrageously enough to require both parents. And plus I just can't let her be the martyr. We share that title.

New Dads, one of the biggest mistakes that families make when going out to dinner is going at the wrong time. If your child goes to bed at 8:30 every night then you have no business being seated in a restaurant at 7:30. Odds are that by the time the main courses arrive you child will be very cranky, fidgety and maybe even loud. Instead, try to be at the restaurant well in advance, in this case between 5:30 and 6 when service should be faster because the dinner crowd hasn't fully descended on the place yet. This will give you a couple of hours of cushion before the bedtime crankiness set in.

If you know that your child is prone to tantrums no matter the time of the day, try to get an outdoor table when possible and appropriate, or a table near a usable exit. This way if your kid does lose it for no reason, you can run him outside quick and easy. You won't disturb the other patrons trying to enjoy their dinners and you can bring him back once he's calmed down.

When you get there, most places will immediately offer a high-chair, depending on the size of your child. If this does not happen, ask the waiter or the host for one. Once seated, this is where you, New Dad, can become a real hero: Pull out the coloring book and washable crayons that you smartly packed. Do not wait for your child to start acting bored and restless—present the first toy as soon as everyone is settled. A lot of family restaurants will have a placemat to color on with some cheap crayons, but don't wait for those things to be offered. Go for yours first and use theirs as a backup if necessary. When the coloring gets old, sing a song (the ABC's are always a good choice), count, play patty cake, and put together a small puzzle. Basically do whatever it takes to entertain the baby until the food comes. But keep it quiet and respect those around you. Your baby may not follow that rule, but you can.

There is a strong possibility that no matter what you do, your child won't be in the mood to be at a restaurant and that's OK. Have whatever you ordered wrapped up and try it again when you feel up to it. It's not a big deal. As dads we tend to envision how an event should go and when it doesn't go as planned, we get frustrated. Frustration is normal, but don't take it to heart. Move onto the next thing and try to socialize your youngster as much as possible while they are young.

Remember, no one knows your child better than you. Modify my advice as you see fit, consult with your co-parent if you have one, and have a great dinner!

4. WIN OR LOSE, WE'RE FATHERS—Winning isn't everything in parenting, but losing isn't an option.

If your toddler is anything like mine, and I suspect he or she is, you are constantly being challenged by your little person to react. You probably find yourself asking the question "Is he trying to piss me off?" The short answer is yes.

Your kid *does* want to see you angry and agitated. But he also wants to see you laugh and smile. Basically they don't care much about what the reaction is, positive or negative—they just want a reaction. It's part of their way of discovering the world and you. Trust me, I understand that this idea is not comforting when your youngster is standing in front of you with sweat and tears streaming down his face, screaming his lungs out with such force that he pukes on your work shoes—all because he wanted to drag an Elmo doll, a Thomas the Tank Engine toy, and a piano to the car when all you wanted to do was pick up dinner.

In that situation, which is oddly similar to one I was in not too long ago, you have a choice to make. You can:

a.) Join in the madness and try to intimidate her into stopping by doing some screaming of your own. You are louder and stronger than her aren't you?

b.) Try to reason with him, and explain why you can't bring so many toys on such a brief outing. You are smarter than him, right?

c.) Put your foot down and not go pick up dinner at all. You don't have to eat *every* night, do you? Gandhi often fasted in protest and he was one of the greatest men that ever lived.

Obviously none of these are very good options. In fact I'm not convinced that there is a good option. All I know is that some battles are not worth fighting and this may be one of them. You have to let it ride out until your little menace tires herself out or gives up, so long as her safety and the safety of those around her are not in any way compromised. My son likes to throw anything that he can get his little hands on when he's angry, so I clear the area of possible projectiles and hope for the best.

I am a bit surprised by how my wife and I handled my son's tantrum. Let's just say that we ended up with all three toys in the car and a toddler that was totally unaware that there was a problem with how he achieved his goal. We, however, were acutely aware of the fact that we had lost the battle—and it was in part because we were not prepared to fight it. We have never seen ourselves as the type of parents that would let our child get the best of us like all those quote unquote "bad parents" out there, but somehow we did. After five long days of working and commuting we just didn't have it in us to go to battle with a professional toddler.

One of the most button-pushing parts of the ordeal was that by the time we reached the car he was talking and laughing and pointing at the buses and cars up the block. It was like nothing ever happened. The problem with that is that something did happen. Two year olds have very good memories, although they'd like you to believe they don't, and if something worked once you had better believe they will try it again. The next time he loses his little boy mind, I am not going to give in no matter what. He will be ignored better than anyone has ever been ignored before. Puke on my shoes? Go for it kid, I'm a rock. Scream as loud as your little body will allow? Be my guest little guy, I brought earplugs.

The worst part of it all was that his tantrum actually did a number on our moderately good moods. He shifted us from the relief of finally making it to the weekend, to despair and hopelessness because we had no interest in dealing with his behavior and we didn't really know how to. Like you, I fully understand that parenting is a 24-hour job, and like our 9 to 5 jobs that we get paid to do, we sometimes find ourselves dealing with problems that we would rather not deal with. But I'll tell you, on a Friday night that feeling is amplified a hundred times. You start telling yourself that you didn't sign on for this—but you know that you did and just when you begin to wonder if it will ever be easier, you know that it will. It's parenting and it isn't the easiest job in the world, but it is arguably the most fulfilling. So after a bit of silence and pondering our lives my wife and I opted to enjoy the rest of the evening and move on to the food and wine that we had planned on finishing out our week with in the first place. The reality was we would live to battle with the boy another day and that would have to be good enough.

When it was all said and done none of us held a grudge. My son talked to us. And we talked back, for the most part. We were reluctant at first to forgive him for his behavior, thinking that he had to be punished in some way for it; however we knew that ignoring a two year old is kind of mean. I admit that we were slow to warm up, but by the time we got home we were all friends again. Somewhere during the evening between the vomit and a round of Old McDonald we decided to give up on the idea of an elaborate meal and grabbed a pizza instead. He ate along with us and afterwards I read him "The Cat in the Hat." When he put his head on my shoulder as we watched the same dragon cartoon that he loves for the one-millionth time, I quickly remembered why I loved being a father.

I guess my point is that we are the adults. We can choose how to handle even the most annoying situation. We can be consistent and unflinching with our demands as long as we are also reasonable and patient. We can also be conscious of our own feelings and not allow our children to stress us out or make us want to strangle them in anger. That, my friends, would be very, very bad. Our kids are works in progress and so are we. I recently told a friend of mine about the fatherhood work that I do and she said to me in all seriousness and sincerity that I must be a great dad. My reply was "I'm actually a terrible father; I just *want* to be a great father." I am sure that you guys out there know exactly what I mean.

5. STEP UP WHEN THE KID IS SICK—Caring for a kid with a bad cold can be a rewarding bonding opportunity.

One of the most difficult things that we can do as fathers is try balance family and work responsibilities and not have one suffer for the sake of the other. Many of us guys feel like just going to work is enough to fulfill our family responsibilities. Meaning, supporting our family financially is all we really need to do. We sometimes think this even when our co-parent also works full-time. This model is obviously flawed.

In my opinion one of the best ways to bond with your child is to volunteer to stay home with her when she's sick with an ear infection, a cold, or if you're really ambitious, the flu. I know it can be difficult to grasp the concept that caring for a sick child is a good thing, so bear with me. Now, I get that there are a lot of negatives to staying home. To start with, you have to use either a personal day, a vacation day, or lose a full day of pay. These things, especially the cash, can be difficult to part with, so use your judgment as to the feasibility and timing of taking time off. Then there's the fact that if you stay home with a sick kid, you run the very real risk of getting sick yourself. I'll be the first to tell you that it's not fun to have to deal with all the stuff that comes along with being away from work for a few days because you have a cold.

Having to play catch-up on a project, missing a deadline, or leaving your staff unsupervised are all very possible. Then there is the reality that there may be no other care options and everything I just said is irrelevant. Nevertheless, I still think staying home with your sick child is a good thing because believe it or not the positives outweigh the negatives.

I first took the day off to care for Devin when he was two. I felt kind of obligated to do it being that the previous day his mother left work early, picked the kid up from daycare, took him to the pediatrician, went and got his prescription filled, all before I got home from work and with the sick baby in tow. So I volunteered to hold down the fort the next day. I've stayed home with him when he was sick in the past, back when he was younger and easier to manage, and I went into it thinking it'd be like the good ol' days when he'd sleep all afternoon and sit quietly on my lap when he was awake. I figured I could get in a little "All My Children" and maybe some "General Hospital." I'd just have to make sure that the juice and toast flowed. As it turned out, caring for the sick two year old toddler version of Devin was noticeably different than caring for the pre-terrible twos Devin.

First of all, his 101-degree fever seemed to energize him. He was like that character from the Fantastic Four, the one they call the Human Torch—just fired up. He didn't want to sit down, anywhere, not on my lap, not on the sofa, not in his booster chair. He was determined to play with his toys and he coerced me into a couple of games of hide and seek. I tried to remind him that he had a fever and an ear infection, but he acted like he didn't know what I was talking about and he kept on trying to enjoy his time away from daycare. The only problem was that Devin was also cranky. So in between the 2,632 books he insisted I read and a few hundred games of imaginary bus, he had several emotional meltdowns.

OK, tantrums.

When your kid is sick you may find it hard to be a disciplinarian as I did. I was all prepared to be a loving nurturing father, yet the kid had no interest in allowing me to do that. He wanted to play and argue and boss me around. With his face encrusted in a snot mask, and a scowl across his face, he pushed me over to the DVD player and insisted on Dragon Tales over Elmo, he slid down the back of our leather sofa and kicked me in the back telling me to get him some milk, and threw the a book at me and told me to read it. When I didn't hop to reading the book fast enough, and opted to look at him like he was crazy instead, he kicked me. That's when I realized that he needed a nap. I gave him a dose a cough syrup, which he promptly spat in my face, and then he plopped down and fell soundly asleep.

When Devin woke up he was in a much better mood. He ate a little something and we had a few civilized interactions while watching TV and reading. His fever broke as he slept, and with it his mean streak. On that particular day there was construction going on outside our apartment window so I took the opportunity to teach him about the different types of equipment, which always fascinates him. He learned about dump trucks, bulldozers, back hoes, cement mixers and other construction equipment. He also belted out the colors of each vehicle and waved goodbye when one of them left the construction site. He, being adorable and rested, helped me get back to being the dad I wanted to be that day. He even gave me a random unsolicited hug. He smeared snot on my jeans in the process, but it was worth it. Kids are moody and unpredictable and we love them in spite of it.

Besides spending meaningful one-on-one time with your tyke, if you are very, very, lucky your co-parent will think you are amazing, dedicated, nurturing, and in turn may be willing to pay you for your services in creative ways. Or he or she may just think you were doing your job and all you'll end up with is a statement like: "So you've been home all day and you didn't even make the bed. I guess I'll do it." Regardless of the outcome, staying home with your kid and your kid being in one piece at the end of the day is a win for fathers everywhere.

6. COMMUNICATION—A good foundation for communicating starts in the early childhood years.

In order to truly understand someone you have to listen to them, even when you don't want to, or should I say, especially when you don't want to. In "The Seven Habits of Highly Effective People" Stephen Covey advises us to listen twice as much as we speak—although, I'm not sure if that idea will translate well to parenting a toddler (you have to talk to toddlers continuously if you want to get them talking). Try thinking of your head as one big ear. Listening is an essential part of two-way communication, even if the person you're trying to communicate with is a toddler.

Small children want to communicate in the language of their caregivers. I'm certain that if my son was raised by wolves, he'd be howling at the moon by now. But he's not being raised by wolves; he's being raised by two new parents, one of which is me. And I'm a new dad that often has no clue what the hell his son is talking about. I know this often-hilarious lack of understanding is normal. It takes years to become a great communicator and lots of people will never be great—just good enough to nail an interview or write a memo. Oscar

Keith Devin Morton

Wilde wasn't two years old when he started spouting Victorian prose and Nas became a hip-hop icon well after finishing the terrible twos. From what I understand there is a very wide range of "normal" when it comes to child development, so I am in no way concerned with the current level at which my son Devin and I communicate. However, that doesn't mean that I don't wonder what motivates him to say what he chooses to say on those days when I do understand him.

During one babbling phase, Devin started saying "Mommy stupid" in daily conversation. It was usually out of the blue, although he sometimes said it when he was asked a question involving his mother. People thought that it was me that he was getting it from and that he was just mirroring what he was being taught. Now, I'll call my wife lots of things like annoying, moody, or even crazy (in a playful way), but I have never called her stupid (and unless things really take a turn for the worse I probably never will). So then the question that needed to be answered was: "How did he come up with that phrase?"

The answer became clear as time progressed and I started listening to both my son and my wife a little closer. What I found was that since my wife doesn't use profanity of any kind, Devin was repeating one of the surrogate profane words that she uses all of the time and that word was "stupid." He was never calling her stupid, I'm sure he doesn't even know what it means, he was simply stating that his mother uses the word "stupid" a lot, hence his phrase "mommy stupid." Lucky for me he repeats much more of what his mother says than what I say because if he repeated what I say we'd have a miniature Martin Lawrence on our hands. My wife has since taught Devin to say "mommy beautiful," instead of what he used to say. We like to call it positive reprogramming.

We are also working on more pressing issues in regards to his language development and speech. For some reason he tends to leave out the "L" in many of the everyday words that he likes to use. This coupled with him being at the stage in life where he shouts out the name of everything he sees, makes for interesting outings. For example, let's say we're at the supermarket and he sees a clock. He then shouts out the word…Or he sees the American flag flying in the park. He shouts out the word…Guys, we're working on it. I promise we are.

Staying on the topic of language development, parents play a major role in this area and should not downplay or disregard it. It's our voices that they hear when they go to bed and wake up in the morning and that is nothing to take lightly. I'm no anthropologist, but what seems to happen is that in daycare, children instinctively form a primitive tribe-like unit with a culture and hierarchy all its own. I am often amazed when I drop off Devin at daycare by how he and his friends all say the same things and speak approximately the same comedic toddler language. That's where we as parents come in.

If we want our kids to speak well, we have to spend lots of quality time with our young children just talking to them. Telling them what we are doing, what we will be doing, and what we just did are examples of topics that will get your child's language development on the right track. It helps them to develop their language skills and to better understand the world.

We also have to give them a chance to speak. They are often saying something insightful or just funny and it's up to us to decipher their language and help develop it. One of the best ways to get your child talking, or closer to it, is by discussing the events of the day at bedtime. It'll be a mostly one-sided conversation at first, but you'll be amazed by how your child will start contributing to the conversation if you are consistent with the bedtime ritual.

So what's your child thinking about? Simple: he's spouting out whatever it is that you are talking about mixed in with some of his random thoughts and words he picked up during the course of his busy day being a toddler.

7. RESPONSIBILITY—Take responsibility for all of your parenting faux pas and move on.

One of the most significant things that we can do as dads, as men, and as human beings for that matter, is know when to take responsibility for our actions, or our lack of action as the case may be.

We live in a time when people are allowed to place blame on others. "I was scalded by a cup of coffee because no one told me it was that hot." "I was fired from my job because my boss never liked me." "I will never be a good dad because my co-parent won't let me do anything my way." The list goes on and on. We never stop to say "hey, most coffee is hot I should have known better," or "I did drop the ball on three important projects," or "I will talk to my co-parent about how important it is for me to actively participate in my child's life." Of course everything isn't your fault. I don't want to get emails from you guys saying stuff like "I used an aerosol hairspray every day for most of the eighties and I am responsible for global warming" or "I watch 'Desperate Housewives' every week just to ogle Eva Longoria and as a result of my watching my wife makes me sleep on the sofa." Neither of those are things you have any control over. It's not your fault the eighties was all about big hair and that Eva is so gorgeous.

This theory holds true in every aspect of our lives, even in being a dad.

One morning my wife and I were very busy with our mischievous little toddler who was in unusually rare form. After changing Devin's diaper my wife grabbed the baby wipes and the soiled diaper and ritualistically put those things in their proper place. The only problem was that she forgot to take the baby powder. My wife and I both know that leaving an open container of powder within reach of Devin is a definite no-no, yet somehow it was forgotten. I had kind of glanced at the powder in the room with him, but was too preoccupied with whatever it was that I was doing to think too much about it. It just didn't click. Two seconds later the clean room I had passed by moments earlier without a thought looked like a crime scene. There was an Elmo chalk outline on the floor and my son looked like Al Pacino in the last few minutes of the movie "Scarface."

All I could do was smile because we are the parents and we had to endure the aftermath of a harmless oversight on our part. My wife was a bit more distraught than I was, letting me know that kids have smothered themselves to death in baby powder. I had never heard that one before—I'm going to write it off as an urban legend, the dramatic ranting of an overworked mother, just so I can stay sane. I'm sure it's possible.

Anyway, I dusted the kid off and vacuumed the floor. I even gave Elmo a couple of whacks across the face—to get the powder off, of course.

It was probably our fault, we know all too well about our child's fascination with baby powder, but it got me to wondering how many kids have done the same thing and were punished for it. I also wondered if maybe he should have been punished for making my living room look like a snow globe. Whose fault was it?

Upon greater scrutiny I am not quite sure. He has played in powder on a much lesser scale in the past and we have told him that he shouldn't. At what point are we to expect our teaching and rules to sink into the toddler mind? I do believe that in this instance Devin should not have been left alone with the temptation of one of his favorite mess makers. But what about the next time?

Well the next time came sooner than I would have expected.

About 45 minutes later...

My family and I live in a small apartment in New York, as is commonplace. Our kitchen doubles as the dining room and is what a real estate agent might call cozy. I was hard at work preparing my famous cinnamon vanilla pancakes, my son was at the kitchen table eating cereal, and my wife was sorting through the mail. We were doing the family thing in the kitchen and just kind of enjoying each other's company.

As Shalawn took three steps over to the garbage can to discard a notice letting us know that we may have just won a new car, I went to the stove to flip a pancake. Literally two seconds later, we turned around and the kid was covered in self-rising flour. I had left the flour on the table. (My secret to really good pancakes—self rising flour Devin looked surprised by what had happened and Shalawn and I were experiencing a strong case of déjà vu. This time the kid was sentenced to some alone time. It wasn't exactly a punishment—he had to go so his mother could clean up the mess—but he took it hard.

We are very strict about misbehavior in the kitchen because the kitchen can be very dangerous for a small child. We expect Devin to be seated at all times when in the kitchen. That's the only way he can be in the kitchen. If he wants to walk around, then he has to go. It's just that simple. But what if he is seated in the acceptable fashion and he decides to act up a little? He has to go. So I guess us putting him out *was* a punishment.

Even though it was my blunder that I left the flour within his reach, it was his fault that he decided to misbehave in the kitchen and play in it. He has been ejected from the kitchen for playing in his juice, throwing food, hopping in his chair, tossing his placemat to the ground, pulling down the curtains, spitting out his food, ripping up his napkin, yelling, turning over his plate and countless other things, so for the sake of consistency, he had to go. This was one time that we could share the blame. I could be wrong though. I'm not Superdad.

My point is that sometimes a kid misbehaves because we as parents make it too tempting for them to not go a little nuts. We know our kids well, that's what separates good dads from all other dads. We know that if our child loves Oreos more than they love their own mother, we shouldn't leave them alone in a room with an open package. And we should know that if we do commit such a blatant faux pas that it's not the fault of the toddler that sees it as an opportunity to see how many cookies she can stuff in her mouth before you get back. In those situations we have to learn the lesson and move on. Punishment may or may not be appropriate, but you have to make that call and try to be consistent with all your other rules.

8. THE POWER OF HUGS— Hugs and love can calm an irate child.

Let's talk about my secret weapon—the HUG. Yes, you read correctly, I said I want to talk about hugs. Do any of you remember the first time you were hugged? We all remember our first kiss, the first time we rode a bike, our first paycheck. Yet, like your first step and your first word, the first hug is long forgotten. A hug is one of the most common and basic human interactions that I can think of. It can send countless messages without you saying a word. A hug can mean glad to see you, I'm sorry for your loss; I love you, goodbye, "wassup," or any combination thereof. A hug can be two bodies coming together and completely connecting in a very intimate embrace, or it can be more formal where just upper bodies touch and hearty pats on the back are exchanged. You can even have a group hug. No matter how you do it, hugs communicate a positive feeling of comfort, support, closeness and familiarity.

So, what the heck does this have to do with being a father? A lot, actually.

Most often when a father hugs his child it's one of those "way to go!" or "aren't you the cutest little thing!" or "show me where it hurts" hugs and is spontaneous. We don't really plan on hugging our kids; we just do it and move on. The child's response is usually a smile, sometimes a giggle and she walks away from the moment feeling loved and comforted. But you can never fully appreciate the true power of a hug until you make a conscious decision to give your child a hug the next time she is totally out of control in the throes of a tantrum. In my opinion the hug's power seems to be more potent when you don't really know why your kid won't stop screaming. It is also powerful when you know the source of your child's erratic behavior yet somehow you cannot verbally convince her that you understand her feelings.

Here's an example of a situation where the HUG might work:

It's a beautiful Saturday morning, and your little living breathing alarm clock is calling your name. He invites you to get out of your warm bed to play. You graciously accept the invitation because you are good dad, and maybe even husband, and you spend the next hour pushing toy cars and trains around your child's bedroom while your co-parent catches a few more ZZZs. You even harmonize a couple of songs about teapots and wheels on buses. Inevitably your energized playmate asks for something to eat. You decide that oatmeal is a good, healthy choice and to show good faith you make enough for yourself, too. You and your toddler eat together and you are amazed by how little mess he makes these days when eating. When your bowls are empty and your stomachs full, the kid asks for a cookie. You smile and gently remind him that it is too early in the morning to eat cookies. You ask if he'd like juice or milk instead. He then moves right into the first meltdown of the day, begging for cookies like a starving orphan that didn't just eat a bowl of oatmeal.

Eventually the words "I want cookie" become indecipherable screams and you find yourself at a crossroads with a very important decision to make. You can either punish the kid for wanting a cookie at 9 a.m. by giving him a timeout where he'll scream until he gives up. The other option is to give him a hug and tell him how you know he likes cookies, and you know he is sad and angry that he can't have a cookie, and that you are sorry he feels that way. Personally, I'd go with the hug. Keep in mind that it works best when you hug him until he noticeably calms down, which may take a couple of minutes.

I'm not 100% sure why it works, I'm just confident that it does. I guess it works for the same reason that every other sincere hug works—the physicality of it cannot be denied.

9. MOTHERS DAY—Always celebrate mother's day, even if you hate the mother of your child.

This can be hard to do. Some non-custodial dads have some baby-mama drama and in some instances kids are used as pawns in an emotionally distressing game of chess where no one wins. If this is your life, hang in there and be the bigger person, even if it's one day a year. I know this is easier said than done. For the rest of you, it won't be a problem.

Without the mothers of our children, we simply would not be dads. So on the second Sunday in May, when we are showing love to our mothers, don't forget about those mothers that made us fathers. It doesn't matter if you are still with the mother or not. As long as she is still a real support system in your life and the life of your child, don't forget to thank her this weekend. The mothers of our children have given us a gift to be cherished, and kept safe. The gift is not returnable or refundable, even though we sometimes wish it was.

When I'm throwing the football *at* my kid (he's not so good at catching yet, but loves it when the Nerf football bounces off his body—whatever floats his boat), I can't help but think that I wouldn't be doing that without my wife's unconditional love and support. Her trusting me with the responsibility of being dad is something I do not take lightly. So pop a bottle of Moët, if you are old enough to do so of course, and celebrate the mothers in your life.

10. SMILING—Learn from the joy of your kids.

Personally I don't make it a habit to smile in public. What I find though is when I do get my facial muscles to strain themselves into a grin the outcome is positive.

It's hilarious to see big, hard faced, serious-looking men just melt when a little boy smiles and waves at them. Their features immediately soften and a cheesy grin spreads across their faces. They mostly offer a hearty wave. And sometimes they add a deep-voiced "hi." Early on when my son Devin started waving at strangers I was embarrassed and wished that he would act like a normal New Yorker. It's just not in our nature to smile and wave at people that we don't know, and Devin needed to understand that.

When Devin was three, I briefly spoke to the owner of his preschool, who mentioned to me that every morning he gets a big smile and wave from my son. The way he told it made me think that maybe it wasn't so embarrassing after all. In fact, we all can learn a little something from my son. It takes about two seconds to acknowledge someone with a *genuine* smile. Two seconds. Even with my busy schedule I can spare two seconds. Try it and see if the person smiles back. You never know, you may just make someone's day. (Or you may just get a beat-down if you choose to smile at a beautiful woman who's with her jealous boyfriend. You'll still be able to smile afterward, but with fewer teeth!) Being a decent human being comes easy for children and it seems to be unlearned or forgotten as we grow into cynical adults.

Kids are unsullied by preconditions and perceived social norms, in other words they are better at being human beings than most adults. I'm learning that and watching it play out through the innocent eyes of my son. He smiles because it feels good and we should try to remember that.

11. PLEASE, NO "THANK YOUS"—Don't thank me, thank the babysitter.

I don't want to be thanked for being a dad. It's like thanking a black man for not going to jail, or a priest for not molesting you. It plays on an unfortunate stereotype. Don't thank me for doing what I'm supposed to do.

Recently I spent the entire day alone with my son because my wife went to a barbecue in another state with some former co-workers. We went to the mall and hung out; he smiled and waved at everyone like some bizarre shrunken politician. He's something of a chick magnet, with his chubby cheeks and easy smile. We ate chicken nuggets like guys do, not counting calories. When we finally went home we watched a movie together then he took a nap. I installed Trend Micro's antivirus software. He woke up and I gave him dinner. By the time my wife came home he was in the bathtub. My wife thanked me for taking care of my boy.

Why is it that we get thanked, or some other kind of random praise, when we do our jobs as dads? At work I expect to be thanked, not at home. I'm not a babysitter, or a nanny, I'm a dad. I expect to get praise once a year on that special day in June set aside for the sole purpose of thanking dads. I want my deeds as a dad to be interpreted as mundane, boring, everyday, routine, and not special. I know my wife meant well, but it's time that we get what we deserve for being dads: nothing. My child's giggles when I make fake farting sounds are thanks enough. Oh, and him one day graduating from Columbia's School of Medicine.

12. AVOID BAD ADVICE— Ignore people who criticize rather than help.

Someone at a family function once told me that the reason Devin was misbehaving was probably due to the television shows that he watches. I thought that was quite interesting for many reasons. One reason was that other than the Saturday morning cartoons on CBS ("Dora the Explorer," "Blues Clues," "Little Bill," etc.) that he watches while my wife and I clean, and the occasional "Barney" breaks at daycare, he doesn't watch TV. The only TV in my house is in my bedroom and that thing only goes on after he is in bed for the evening. We don't even have cable. Also, this person insisted that my method of handling his behavior was not satisfactory— telling Devin face to face to calm down and a couple of timeouts was, in her opinion, not enough—apparently Devin needed a beating. This person saw what she thought was unacceptable behavior and decided on an unsolicited punishment. Case closed.

I took several other factors into consideration when I, Devin's father, was deciding on discipline options. One factor was environmental. He was hanging out with a bunch of people that he had either never met, or had met infrequently, in a huge four story house that he rarely visits. In this house that dwarfs our apartment, he was playing with a couple of children that were a little older than him and both were trying to get him to do big kid things, like climb the stairs to the fourth floor. As if that weren't enough he had been up since six-thirty in the morning (he's an early riser) and he did not nap because we had spent the entire day out. To add to an already less than ideal situation he was about an hour away from his normal bedtime! With all of those factors in place I could hardly expect him to act like an angel, and I believe that the way I was disciplining him reflected the uncommon situation and was consistent with how I would have handled him at home.

My point, New Dads, is simple. If you are a parent that spends as much quality time with your offspring as is humanly possible and if you take your role as care-giver and dad seriously, then you know you child better than anyone else. No one can tell you why your child is the way he is, unless the person is a trained profes-sional. And even then, a true professional will likely base most of her analysis on what *you* told her about your child. Be confident in the fact that you know your child's temperament, schedule, thought process and triggers. There are several tried and true behavior mod-ification techniques, like hugs, which work on children, but the only time they really work is if you know when to use them. And knowing when to use them comes from knowing your child.

There will always be people that believe that they know what's right for and wrong with your kid. Some of these people will give you their unsolicited opinion on your parenting style to your face, while others will talk about you behind your back. However understand that you know your child better than anyone else and that's the only thing that matters.

13. GIVE PRIORITY TO SLEEP— Sleeping half the day isn't a bad thing when you're young and growing.

Parents make all kinds of excuses about why their kids don't have regular bedtimes. They talk about how their kids aren't tired at 7:30 at night, or that their kid is fine with only eight hours of sleep. There are even parents who claim they won't be able to spend any time with their kids if they put them to sleep too early—that's hard and I can relate. I get home at 6:30 p.m. and my son goes to bed at about 7:30. Not even Superdad can add minutes to a day no matter how much they are needed. An hour is just not enough time to wind down from the busy day and connect with your family, I'll concede that. Still, you must make the best decision for your child's growth and development. Sleep saved my family so I suppose I'm a little biased. Getting enough sleep each night made my son ready to take on the world every day by improving his mood, giving him energy, and providing structure.

I'll probably say this in some way, shape or form in the future because I strongly believe it's important: little kids need lots of sleep! Sometimes we forget that just because a child can stay up until 9, 10, or later doesn't mean they should. Small children need something like 10 to 12 hours of sleep every night. Yes, your little unemployed mooch should spend about half their day sleeping. No, they don't care that you have worked all day. They have no shame. The reality is that sleep is when a child's developing mind sorts through and recovers from a day of processing all the new information that they took in. Also, sleep helps to prevent attention problems (and anything that may help to limit the possibility of another one of our babies being labeled with ADD is worth a lot of consideration). So put that kid to bed, and then put yourself to bed, you deserve the rest!

14. PROTECT THE FAMILY AT ALL COSTS—Being poppa bear is just part of the job.

It's probably not a good idea to debate with your wife over who goes into the house first when there are guns in full view on your street. Know when to debate and when not to.

One evening, I was coming in the house with Devin and Shalawn after a long day of work and driving for an hour through some of the worst thunderstorms I've seen in a long time (with the gas tank on "E" most of the way). As we walked up to our front door, I noticed two big juicy snails sliding along the stoop. I took a second to point them out to my son. He looked on with mild amusement as I explained that a snail carries his home on his back and moves slowly from place to place because it has no legs or feet. My lame attempt at a science lesson was cut short when I heard yelling in the background—and my wife saying, "Get in the house."

In the street, a police officer stood, with gun drawn, cocked, and aimed, screaming at a man to get out of his van. I fumbled for my keys and finally got the door open. I was concerned that a shootout would jump off and insisted my wife and child go in the house first.

Keith Devin Morton

"No you go, I'll get the door," My wife urged.

I said, "Just go on, I'll worry about the door." She would not, and we went back and forth a couple of times until I relented and pulled Devin inside with me. She followed.

I could not believe that we had to argue to decide who would go inside the house to safety first. My logic had been that I'm the man of the house and if anyone was going to get shot, it would be me. She was saying to herself, logically, that she could close the door faster because she didn't have anything in her hand as I had. All the bickering in another, more volatile situation might have gotten us all killed. If I've learned anything from living in rough neighborhoods over the years it's that most people can't shoot straight, not even the police.

That being said, a man, especially a black man, has to be allowed to protect his family as he sees fit and our women should try to respect that when it makes sense. Next time she goes in first with the boy. I'm counting on there not being a next time, but you never know.

15. KIND WORDS FROM THE DEVIL—Sometimes they find the words to tell you they appreciate you, so listen closely.

One evening, my wife decided to brave the Manhattan crowds in search of the perfect Christmas-themed bathroom curtains, and I was left alone with Devin. Despite the millions of hours I have spent alone with our child, I still have to convince my wife that we will be fine without adult supervision. Yes, in my mind I'm saying, "Oh God please don't leave me alone with… him!" However the words that come out of my mouth are always, "Would you just leave? I know how to take care of our son." Anyway, she was gone and Devin and I were bonding—I was pulling him off of stuff and giving him timeouts, he was calling me names and being mischievous. The usual. Then he asked for dinner. I agreed it was time to chow down. I set a pot to boil and he immediately insisted that it was hot and that I should add the noodles. I told him that the water wasn't hot yet and he pouted a bit. Then he called my name. I prepared for another cooking lesson from my tiny chef.

"Daddy!"

"Yes, Devin?"

"You're a good daddy."

"What?" I couldn't hide my amazement.

"You're a good daddy," he repeated with a toothy smile.

"Thank you Devin. That means a lot coming from you." I meant it.

Maybe three minutes later he said "Shut up, Daddy, before I hit you in the mouth," because he was tired of me singing Christmas songs. Good thing I'm a good daddy because had I done to him what first came to my mind I would have been a very, very bad daddy.

16. YOU MUST ADDRESS BACKTALK—No matter how amusing, backtalk is disrespectful—address it all consistently.

Not too long ago, I was picking up Devin from daycare when I had a real ah-ha moment. I have quite a few of those moments, but this one was particularly disturbing because I should have seen it for what it was long ago. I was helping the boy tie his sneakers at daycare, and as we were going over the many events of the day I overheard a familiar conversation that most parents have had, or will have, with their two or three year olds. The teacher that was supervising the dismissal of the group asked this normally sweet little girl that I have known since she was six months old to sit down in her chair. The little girl promptly replied "No you sit down in the chair." What happened next floored me. It hit me like a ton of bricks, actually. The teacher said in a stern and authoritative voice, "Megan, don't talk back to me. Sit down in your chair."

Ah-ha! All those times that Devin has said a single word after I told him to do something (or not to do something as the case often is), he was not merely asserting his personality—the little tyrant was talking back! It is a phrase that came rushing back to me from my childhood and I realized that I had mistaken his protests for something other than what they were. It was outright backtalk, nothing more and certainly nothing less.

Instead of identifying the act and addressing it, I had simply repeated my command, or physically made him do something. I was allowing him to have somewhat of a say, but once you allow a child to get in a single word, it becomes an argument, and under no circumstances do you ever argue with a toddler. We are the parents, what we say, as long as we have the best interest of our children in mind, goes. Case closed.

The trouble is that it is sometimes difficult to identify a behavior for what it is, especially if it is your first time as a parent. Sometimes a kid jumping up and down on a bed having the time of her life giggling and carrying on can be the cutest thing in the world, until you realize that her motor skills are still developing and it's a very real possibility that she will lose control of her romping and go flying off of the bed and onto the floor. It is impossible to have all the bases covered and have a full grasp of every possible scenario that you may face. But as fathers and caregivers, we have to cover as many bases as we can.

I'm sure that some of you think that I am nuts for not recognizing this backtalk behavior earlier on, but as they say, the first step is admitting you have a problem. Ever since that day, I have been consistently on Devin about it and he has been responsive. My guess is that part of his turnaround comes from the fact that I am now reinforcing what is being done in daycare. Usually, I'm struggling to get the daycare to reinforce what we are doing at home, but I guess there is a first time for everything.

17. THE RADIO—Be mindful of what's playing on your radio (our kids really do hear everything!).

I love hip-hop. One of my fondest memories as a stressed-out teen was when I was cutting class in high school and The Notorious B.I.G. walked into the pizza shop where I had been eating with another fellow high school slacker. B.I.G.'s red Land Cruiser sat out front, gleaming in the bright Brooklyn sun. He was decked out in a Coogi sweater and Versace shades, the same expensive clothes that he often sang about. He ordered a couple of slices, disappointed his fans by declining to sign autographs, and left. He rode shotgun in the SUV because he notoriously did not have a driver's license. I'll never forget that moment because when he walked in I was nodding my head to "Ready to Die" on my Walkman.

Another time, Jay-Z walked into a movie theater off of Union Square in Manhattan where my friends and I were catching a flick. He was with this gorgeous girl and was looking for a seat. No entourage. Being one of the hottest hip-hop artists on the street, he didn't stay long because people started harassing him. Fans all over the auditorium kept shouting "Jigga," a nickname he was using at the time. We just hoped he'd sit next to us. "In My Lifetime Vol. 1" had just dropped. We almost crapped ourselves just by being in the same room with him.

I was a fan of B.I.G. and Jay long before they were legends. And I still am. I want to share hip-hop with my son. Edited, radio-ready hip-hop. I know I can't play "Illmatic" for a three year old, but I should be able to listen to the regular radio with him in the car. However, it is becoming increasingly difficult to do that. Since no one has cracked down on "bitch" or "ass," I can't seem to turn on the radio without hearing the two in heavy rotation. Why do I have to be called a "bitch" by a DJ? I don't think that it's a very nice greeting. Why can't I listen to the radio anymore without being cursed out?

I wish hip-hop radio would tone it down so that the future generations of fans don't have to feel like they have to be vulgar to be cool. I already stopped listening to morning shows on the radio for the sake of my son's vocabulary. Please don't make me turn off the radio for the rest of the day, or worse—go to pop music radio.

18. VACATION!—Take a break from the everyday grind whenever it makes sense financially and emotionally.

Everyone should plan to take a break from the day-to-day. A change of scenery may be all that you need to recharge your batteries and preserve your sanity. If you plan well and save, a good vacation may be on the horizon.

In July 2006, I took a pleasant vacation tlo Myrtle Beach with my wife and three-year-old son. On the advice of my boss, we decided to stay at a condo on the beach. For $150 a night, we got a bedroom, a full kitchen, a balcony and a living room on the 22nd floor of the resort. The resort sat directly across the street from a great little quiet beach. We drove from New York—it's a 12-hour trek, but we laid over in Richmond Virginia each way, because you have to stop a lot with a toddler. We rented a car to avoid raising the odometer 1400 miles on the vehicle we needed for our daily grind, and it got us to many nearby attractions in minutes. "Broadway at the Beach," one of the best parts of the trip, is a huge outdoor entertainment and shopping complex and was about seven minutes away from our hotel.

Keith Devin Morton

The reason this trip worked so well was that during the day we hung out as a family visiting museums, fun houses, amusement parks, miniature golf courses and, of course, the beach. Then when the sun went down my wife and I would sit on the balcony watching the Atlantic Ocean break against the beach, drinking cocktails and reconnecting, all while the kid was sound asleep in the bedroom. The weather was perfect for July, and our toddler was on his somewhat best behavior. Devin was sentenced to time out a few times and he got grumpy as hell when he was tired from all of the activities, but overall not too bad.

As far as family vacations go, we could not have had a better experience. There were plenty of other families around looking stressed out, but having fun, and the people are very friendly. We even plunked down the debit card for an additional night because we did not want to go home. When planning your vacation, be sure to consider a place that is both family-friendly and romantic. We struck gold with Myrtle Beach.

Oh yeah, almost forgot: We purchased a portable DVD player with a 7 screen for the long journey and a car mounting kit. Smartest thing we ever did to prepare for a trip. But only for a trip, not every day life.

19. GIVE INCENTIVES FOR POOPING—Potty training is one time when bribery may be a really good idea.

For several months, my wife and I tried with very limited success to potty train our less-than-interested son. We had been pulling our hair out trying to determine which potty training approach would be most effective for a child that is obviously intelligent enough to learn how to use a toilet, but otherwise unmotivated. When we consulted magazines and real life professionals, we got answers that vary only slightly in degrees of discouragement. Devin's pediatrician said, "Don't force him. I promise he'll be potty trained by the time he gets married!" Needless to say, Shalawn and I were not amused. I just thought about the diaper and laundry bills from decades of Devin pooping in his pants. It would be sure to have a catastrophic impact on his college fund.

When we thumbed through several parenting magazines, which by the way, always seem to have an unhelpful article on potty training in every issue we were left in a chronic state of melancholy. OK, maybe I'm being a bit hard on the parenting magazines. I guess I want the trick, or the pill or the 100% guaranteed foolproof *thing* that will make my little boy love the idea of taking a dump on the big boy toilet. The reality is that there is no silver bullet solution to the potty training dilemma.

Even the pros cannot agree. One said, you should wait until your child is four if need be, another said they'll go when they are ready, and yet another refused to give an age range for when you should expect your little poo factory to start saving you some money on diapers.

Shalawn and I have recently decided on a course of action and are currently implementing it. It's a gently encouraging technique that uses stickers as the prize for completing various stages of the potty process. A colleague gave me the suggestion after having marked success with her daughter and using these very special glitter and gel-like stickers that excited the little girl. The little girl was allowed to stick these stickers all over the bathroom door after she won them and loved looking at them as a reminder of her success. Eventually she no longer needed stickers as encouragement to use the bathroom because to her and her parents using a diaper was no longer an option.

For us to implement "operation sticker," we had to decide on a sticker style that would be special to Devin. So I ordered 600 Thomas the Tank Engine reward stickers. Like so many little boys, Devin loves that little blue train! We also use a different set of stickers to encourage overall good behavior. If he had a very good morning or afternoon, or behaved well during an outing we give him a sticker. As far as the potty training goes the results have been much more encouraging than some of the other aforementioned advice. At first we would give him a sticker for sitting on the toilet and trying to go, or for washing his hands. Then we moved onto telling him that he was so good at trying to go and washing his hand that all the stickers for that were gone and now he had to earn the pee pee stickers.

Who knows if he understood us—he only knew then that he had to show us proof if he wanted a sticker. As a result, he started doing number one on the toilet somewhat frequently, though number two was still a challenge. Someone (Freud?) once told me that little people think of their poo as part of them and are horrified to see it flushed away. It's a funny thought even if it's probably not true.

The reality is that those annoyingly helpful magazines and experts are right: there is no magic potty pill. Potty training is all about trial and error and your child's personal readiness. I know some parents that have children that hate to be dirty in any way, so all they did was put big-kid underwear on their child and in an effort to stay clean the kid started using the potty. I have known other people that were so poor that they could not afford diapers; therefore they worked with their babies, non-stop to make sure that they understood that the potty was the place to be. I also have known parents, and this smug group is the one I don't like much because I'm the jealous type, where the kid was just ready to use the potty at 18 months and there was no training involved. You may find that doing the pee pee dance and singing the pee pee song is all that your kid needs to get the old juices flowing—it's trial and a lot of error. There are so many ways to potty train a kid and so many signs that they are ready to use the potty that it just goes back to the old adage that you know your child best. So good luck in figuring out what works and know that I am with you in the struggle!

20. SURVIVING VULGARITIES—Filthy language can be a problem, even if you don't curse at home, but don't panic.

Devin's cursing phase is one for the record books. But thankfully, one day it just clicked with him and now he's the voice of reason. He'll even call out grown men on the subway for cursing around him. He thinks that cursing is uncivilized and I'm glad for it. A couple of years ago, though, he wasn't so classy.

My son didn't do stand-up comedy, but he did use much of the same language made famous by the late great Richard Pryor in his heyday. He usually gets crazy when he's sleepy and all of his defenses are down, however on occasion he'll drop the F-bomb just to piss his parents off. Most people think I'm full of crap when I say this but I'll say it anyway: he discovered his hidden potty mouth somewhere else other than home.

I'm sure you won't believe this, but I don't curse around my boy, and my wife hasn't uttered a single vulgarity in the six years we've been together. We don't even watch R-rated or PG-13 DVDs until he's snoring in his bedroom. Yet, somehow when he's pissed and

Keith Devin Morton

tired he'll tell his parents to "shut the fuck up," which is often code for something as simple as letting us know it's time for bed. The problem is that most people in the street aren't as conscious of what they say as my wife and I. I am acting high and mighty on this topic because we take it very seriously, and we don't curse. I think that's the reason why his cursing pushes our buttons so much (beyond the fact that a three year old should never know how and when to use the F-word).

One of the most difficult things about being a parent is that you can't police caregivers or other parents. You just have to hope that common sense wins out in the majority of circumstances so that your child is not exposed to age-inappropriate things. During Devin's cursing phase, my mother told me about a little rumor that was buzzing around my son's preschool involving me (my mother is the head teacher in the infant room so she knows all the teachers). Apparently my son has told all of his caregivers that his "daddy says bad words" to him. I wasn't surprised by this because the nice ladies that care for him had been looking like they wanted to tell me something all week. He informed them that I tell him to "shut the fuck up." It's actually quite funny in a horrifying kind of way. Any father that says that to their kid should not be a father, much less a father fighting the good fight. Nonetheless, I can see my boy telling the story of my alleged obscenity-filled tirades with the seriousness of a doctor explaining to a patient that he has three weeks to live.

My son is good at the straight-faced delivery of a bold-faced lie. And he's only three! Maybe he does need a sibling as so many people have told me and my wife. (Not gonna happen.) And it appears that he will tell anyone with a pulse and a pair of ears that his dad curses him out like a dog. One morning I had to call home from the supermarket because I forgot why I was there. My wife did not hear the telephone, but Devin sure did. He picked up the phone and the conversation went something like this:

"Hello," he said

"Devin, is that you? Where's your mother?" I asked.

"My daddy says bad words to me."

"Boy, this is your daddy and I have never done such a thing. Where's mommy?"

"She's doing something. My daddy said to me…."

"Don't you dare say it!"

"Here, Mommy, somebody's on the phone."

Then he handed the phone over to his mother. The kid is out to get me. He wants to defame me. He wants to make me look like a bad father. Damn he's good.

21. "I HATE YOU, DADDY!"— Don't believe everything kids say when it comes to emotions of the heart.

It's a new phrase that my kid picked up from the infamous *somewhere*. Perhaps I should be glad that he's expanding his vocabulary and expressing himself. He uses it whenever he doesn't get his way, which lately seems often. Of course he says those four words to get a rise out of me, and has no clue what they really mean, but that doesn't make it any less annoying. He sounds like a spoiled rich kid, which is ironic because as far as I can tell he's broke. My boy is a hater. And like Mary J. Blige says, "We don't need no hateration." I'm proud of the fact that he speaks very well for a three year old (I'm around shrunken people a lot in my work, so I know). Nevertheless, the kid chooses some of the worst words EVER to practice his annunciation.

22. LESSONS LEARNED—The road our kids end up taking isn't always the one they start on.

Certain news events can be sobering, if not distressing. And on occasion, a news story can resonate in a way that you wouldn't have expected. There are a variety of reasons for this, only one of which is that you're acquainted with the subject of the story.

A young man that I went to junior high school with was arrested on gun possession charges linked to the murder of a NYC municipal worker. The school that we went to was for so-called "gifted and talented" students. It was small, about eight classes all together, so we all knew each other. The fact is that I haven't seen the guy for almost two decades and where I'm from, this kind of thing happens almost every day. I've lost more than my share of friends and former classmates to either prison or death. Nevertheless, for some reason this guy's arrest kindled something within me. We were destined to become the cream of the crop. We were the chosen ones, and we had the standardized test scores to prove it.

Yet, somehow, too many of us lost our ways. Some of us had children very young and couldn't keep our grades up while supporting our children. Some of us went to jail for petty crimes and ruined our chances of going to college. Others of us simply were dragged down by the weight of poverty, and the influences of the street. A few of us just gave up. Our parents (lots of mothers, few fathers) did the best they could with what they had, so I can't fault them. They tried.

I think about my son and all the ways his life can be derailed. The thought sets me on edge, and motivates me at the same time. I know that if I leave him and allow the streets (or plain old laziness) to swallow him up I'll never be able to live with myself. It actually amazes me how many dads can walk away from their children. To me, walking away from my son would be like deciding that I no longer need air or water to live. I don't know if my former classmate had a dad that loved and supported him, but I know that my son does. I hope that it's enough.

23. REWARD GOOD BEHAVIOR—Rewarding good behavior is more effective than bribing a kid to stop naughty behavior.

Earlier in this book I asked, "Does your child really want to piss you off?" and the answer was a resounding yes. And as our children get older, the answer is still yes. The only difference is that a three- or four-year-old has better command of the English language than they did at two, and now they will gladly articulate to you where they want you to go and how you should get there. And I'm not talking about them telling you to go on vacation to Hawaii and that you should take an airplane to get there, either. Devin and many of his partners in mischief are surprisingly fearless when it comes to challenging authority. I picture a man three feet taller than me and five times my weight and I personally get a little nervous, but not the average toddler. Yes, we're bigger and we're stronger, and they don't care.

Most kids will calm down over the next couple of years, but that will not help you right this second. Right now is when they want to challenge you, see how far they can push you before you push back, see how hard they can hit you before you hit back, and see how much they can curse you before you curse back. When they see that you are not fazed by any of those things, as Devin has figured out, then they think that they have you under their control. At least until you pull out the famous timeout. An invisible barrier goes up around them and they can't move from the time out chair, corner, mat, stool, or whatever the tool is that you choose for time out. They don't know where you conjured this mighty weapon from and are knocked off balance by it. They try to speak in time out and you say no talking, they try to reach for a nearby toy and you say no playing, they try to stand and you tell them no standing. Sometimes you repeat those lines over and over again, but if you are consistent they listen. This will work most times. Sometimes it will not, but then you have other weapons.

One of the techniques that we are using is rewarding Devin out of the blue for good behavior. If we go to the supermarket and he acts out we don't try to bribe him in the supermarket with goodies, we either remove him from the supermarket and tell him about why we left and then decide on a punishment, or we let him get over his issues on his own. However if he goes to the supermarket and he behaves, then when we get home we remind him of where we went and ask him to recall events from the trip (for example we'll say "Devin, where did we just go?" and "Did you get to sit in the cart?") and then we tell him how great his behavior was at the supermarket and that he deserves to choose a sticker from the treasure chest. He enthusiastically chooses one, we find it later stuck to something in the house and we move on to the next one. On rarified days, if he really outdid himself with politeness, no tantrums, and listening to directions, then we'll go somewhere special to eat chicken nuggets—his absolute favorite—for lunch or dinner.

The problem is that he's starting to make the connection between good behavior and chicken nuggets, so sooner or later we'll have to replace the item or explain to him that he doesn't need nuggets to behave himself, the same way you would start weaning your child off of praise once they are potty-trained. At that point, we'll cross our fingers and hope it worked.

It's a bad idea to train your child to associate goodies and treats with unacceptable behavior. We see it all the time: a stressed parent, usually one of us dads, pleading with a child in the midst of a tantrum and saying those dreadful words "If you calm down I'll buy you an ice cream." That's some sad parenting. Don't go down that road. Instead, buy the kid some ice cream when she actually deserves it and be as clear as you can about how she earned it. I recommend that you focus on behaviors that you really want to change. If your child is a hitter and he doesn't hit you all morning one day, let him know that he didn't hit you all morning and you are proud of him for controlling his temper. Then let him choose a sticker or something from the treasure chest. The same if your child picked up some bad language from daycare. Let the little reforming potty mouth know that you noticed that he has not cursed today and that he's awesome for it. Focus on the positive behavior and maybe the negative behavior will become a thing of the past.

24. ZOOS, GARDENS, AQUARIUMS—Go. And take advantage of coupons.

I cannot deny the draw of an outing to the movies. The movie theater is a controlled environment with 90 minutes or more of guaranteed entertainment. Add some candy, nachos, and soda, and you can have a great two hours even if the movie is not so good. A movie may be a great idea for a date; however I think that kids should be stimulated in more significant ways. Kids should be taken out into the world even if you only do something mundane like see the local sights. The reality is that your small child is a tourist when it comes to hanging out. They haven't seen most of the cool stuff your city or town has to offer, so what's boring to you may be a thrill to them. Don't deprive them of experiences.

We finished off a summer fieldtrip trifecta with a trip to the New York Aquarium. Knowing that my son loses his freaking mind late in the afternoon, we rushed out of the house at about 10:30 a.m. to get an early start and we arrived at the aquarium just in time to check out the sea lion show. My boy didn't drop a single four-letter word and we actually had fun. Usually he's quite the grouch when we try to enjoy an outing, so today was a welcome change of pace. After we got tired of looking at spindly crustaceans and obese walruses, we walked the boardwalk and enjoyed watching all of the exotic looking people Coney Island attracts. However, as usual, I noticed that there were more black families walking the boardwalk than there were in the aquarium. Many more. The same thing was the case at the New York Botanical Garden and the Bronx Zoo I'm not sure if it's an issue of economics, lack of interest, or both. Maybe, the Zoo is thought of as the realm of the white folks. The reality is that it's expensive to go to places where there is knowledge to gain. It must have cost close to $300 in total to hang out at all three places for half a day. That makes it very inaccessible to those that are already unemployed, or the working poor. Yes, there are free days during the week, but that's when people are working to pay the bills.

I wish I could see more black dads out and about teaching their kids about wildlife and exotic plants. I'm allergic to EVERYTHING at the Botanical Gardens, yet there I was, trying to explain what a damn cactus is to a three-year-old. I think the biggest issue is economics, though. It's cheaper and easier to go to a movie matinee that will occupy a kid for two hours, especially after a long week of work. I get that. It sucks and it's sad. Another quiet example of how poor people (which usually means minorities in NYC) get the short end of the stick. Though that seems to be shifting as parents of all races get more savvy about their entertainment and educational options, and understand the importance of seeking out unique experiences.

There are options though. The smaller zoos are kind of cheap and many museums allow entry with just a suggested donation. There are also coupons and special events where you can get the best in educational entertainment without breaking the bank. The key is keeping your eyes open, picking up the free regional and local newspapers and using the Internet to find deals. Sign up for mailing lists at your local area attractions so you can stay on top of what's going on, and when it's free or discounted.

25. DADDY, WHAT'S A NUKE?—Know what's going on in the world—the good, the bad, and the ugly.

I loathe the news. It's often depressing, glorifying violence and frequently depicting black folk as troglodytes. Nevertheless, I feel that as a father I have to know what's going on out there. If I need to be more vigilant on the subway, or get prepared for a big snowstorm, it's the news that helps me decide on a course of action. One of the best things you can do as a father is to stay informed about your world, your country, and your community.

To do this, I suggest that you get your news from more than one source, especially when it comes to international affairs. Living post 9/11, it is imperative that you get a well-rounded perspective on what's going on in the world. Visit international news websites like the BBC, and seek English-language editions of foreign newspapers both online and in print. (I like the *Jamaica Gleaner* for a unique perspective.) This way you can find out what other people are saying about us instead of what we are saying about ourselves. Community newspapers are also a great way to get local information—not only about the serious stuff, but about the best neighborhood hotspots and festivals, too. With the explosion of the Internet, you can find information anywhere, but it is becoming harder to find well-reported, credible news and it's up to you to determine what standards you will settle for when it comes to protecting yourself and your family.

26.HALLOWEEN—Halloween is one of those fun parenting opportunities to be silly and creative. And it only comes once a year.

It's encouraging to know that there are so many of us out there. We are not alone; we are experiencing fatherhood's ups and downs together, and even if our lives do not intersect, they definitely parallel.

Since the birth of my son, I have developed a new appreciation for Halloween. The fun of the day fades with age, but when you have a child, you are reminded of how silly and great Halloween can be. Before my son had an opinion, my wife and I dressed him up as a spider, a dragon, and a pirate. Now we let him choose the costume, which is always fun. He really likes pirates so when he was three, he chose to be one again. I can see the appeal: you can wear a big hat, ripped up pants, carry a plastic sword, and scream "arghhh" at strangers. When you're three years old what's better than that? If your child is old enough to vocalize what they want to be this Halloween, you should go with their suggestion. Your little princess may end up dressed as Spider Man (which happened to a cousin of mine a few years back), or your cute little puppy may want to try on some fangs. Either way it'll be fun.

If you or your partner are particularly skilled in arts and crafts, or are just ambitious, you may want to try your hand at making a costume. There are tons of books on the subject, and just about every national parenting magazine (some of which are free) offers tips on how to do it. A Halloween costume could be a great project to work through with your little one. Think of how much bonding you can do with a little glue and glitter! If you decide to go with a store-bought costume, try to at least get your hands on a fresh pumpkin, so you can carve it into a jack-o-lantern with your kid. That's a project that never gets old and they sell carving kits just about everywhere.

One thing to watch out for, though, is the candy. There's no better time for candy-lovers than Halloween, but we as parents are faced with the challenge of keeping most of these sweets out of our kids' sticky little hands. Some candy, such as jelly beans and caramel-covered popcorn, must be screened because they can become choking hazards for small kids. Another caution candy is chocolate, which has traces of caffeine in it. Chocolate should be eaten in small quantities and *never* before bed—you don't want to find out that your kid is caffeine-sensitive because she is swinging from your track-lighting at 11:30 on Halloween night. Remember that sugar rushes and sugar crashes are real and that you can avoid them if you set clear and consistent ground rules about the consumption of candy. Sweets are proof that there can be too much of a good thing.

27. CHILDREN AND CHARITY—
Teach giving.

I am over a decade into my non-profit career, so I have a real commitment to the idea of charity. I know firsthand that every donation, big or small, helps change lives. When you find a charity that speaks to you, you should try to support it. Good charities can range from a grassroots advocacy group run out of a church basement to a huge, zillion-dollar multi-site social service agency serving many thousands of people—and everything in between. My only advice is for you to do your homework and support the good charities. There are plenty of online resources, such as Charity Navigator and Guide Star who can help you make an informed decision about charitable giving.

My kid never ceases to amaze me. He says the funniest stuff ("Daddy, I'm not going to like you today. Today I'm going to only like Mommy."). He does funny things like dancing "the robot." The amazing part, however, is his willingness to give stuff away. Sure, he'll never give away his trains, but he is still willing to part with items that belong to him. I, being the proud poppa that I am, want to toot his little train whistle for him because he won't toot his own.

We've been preparing our boy for the act of giving some of his new and used things away. Surprisingly, he was on board with the idea from day one. We told him he was going to give some of his clothes, shoes, bedding, and toys to The Salvation Army, a long-time charity of ours. He helped his mother bag up all of his donations into what ended up being seven garbage bags and a car seat. Then, we crammed into our little blue Hyundai and trudged for an hour to our destination. Once there, my little man marched a bag of blankets and bumpers into the warehouse and handed it over with a huge, adorable smile. The staff was very friendly to him, which we liked a lot. Afterwards we talked about all of the people that his donation would help and he was so proud.

Before he went to bed, he asked about all of the kids that would be wearing his clothes and playing with his toys. In response he got a fantastic story about happy children and loving parents enjoying his donation. He went to bed smiling. It was a really good day and we all learned a great lesson about the beauty and importance of charity. I can't wait until Christmas.

28. COLD/FLU SEASON— Strongly consider getting the flu shot and other life-saving vaccinations.

Make sure you vaccinate your little ones. Do the research; ask the right questions if you aren't sure. It may save their lives.

Do you want to know how I discovered that the cold and flu season is a real phenomenon and not something made up by pharmaceutical companies and the CDC? Well here it is: My son simultaneously coughed *and* sneezed into my mouth one morning as I was buckling him into his car booster seat. It tasted pretty much like my own spit and snot, aside from the bits of waffle that were mixed in with it. Yummy. I very kindly said, "Bless you little guy," to which he replied in his ever-pleasant deadpan way, "Leave me alone, Daddy." Oh, I just want to eat him up! The inconvenient irony of the pending illness that's brewing in my boy is that he was scheduled for a flu shot this weekend and now, of course, we are going to have to cancel. As many urban parents know, it's not easy getting appointments with decent doctors.

And my car's check engine light is on.

29. A "HEALTHY FEAR" OF DAD—How healthy can fear be?

I didn't have to go to work one day because of the Christmas holiday, so I left the kid with his great grand-mother and went to the barber shop. It was a lively day at the shop, much more so than usual. We talked about politics, the old-timers talked about the old times, we discussed racism, sports (which I don't know a thing about), down-low brothers (I have no clue why), how messed up the youth are, and a bunch of other stuff. All ages were represented today and many opinions shared in a friendly, respectful way. I, however, was less into the conversation than others because I was focused on the young black dad that was there with his twin sons.

The two little boys were the best behaved 21-month olds I had ever seen. They did not squirm in the barber chair as they got their haircuts. They were patient beyond what you can reasonably expect from children so young. The dad had no toys and did not bribe his kids with food. It was amazing. We chatted for a moment and I found out that the dad was a reverend and on his way to a new church placement in the south. I told him that he was lucky to have such well-behaved children. He said to me:

"I believe that kids should have a healthy fear of their parents. I started working on that very early on."

I had to smile at that. My son has no fear, healthy or otherwise. I always thought that my kid should have a healthy *respect* for me and I'm going to stick with that theory for a little while longer. Fear will be my last resort. The fact is that disciplining small children is hard. Many parents are divided on the idea of spanking vs. non-corporal punishments. Parents have told me that it's much easier to spank a kid and move on than it is to stick to a punishment like making a child go to bed early, or enforcing no desert for a week. They say that spanking shows a little brat who is the boss and builds upon what that barber shop father called a "healthy fear of Dad." I'm not sure there is such thing as a healthy fear of anything, unless we are talking about things like having a healthy fear of, say, bears and tigers, or guns. Otherwise, I think it's a flawed theory. But I'll openly concede that getting a truly irate three-year-old into the naughty chair for timeout is about as easy as trying to herd cats; the same way that attempting to get a habitually back-talking kid to shut his or her stinking mouth is probably about as easy as convincing your boss to give you a $1.6 million dollar raise.

Full-blown spankings should never be your first recourse when a good, structured timeout is possible and appropriate. Allow me to share with you how my wife and I turned disorganized timeouts into structured, meaningful punishments.

First you have to make sure that you have the tools you need to pull it off. Get yourself an egg timer, nothing fancy, just something to count out the minutes.

Second, decide on where the timeouts will be and stick to it. I know a parent that has decided that the first step on their staircase is the "naughty step." Others have a specific corner in their house where the kid must stand. Corners are particularly good because they are kind of portable, you can always find one in public if they need a timeout in a restaurant or store. In my house we use a kid-sized sofa as the naughty seat.

Third, make sure you have lots of patience as you go into the process; it may not work perfectly the first few times.

The real reason why this process works is the egg timer. The timer makes sure that the timeout is a fair length. Dr. Bob Sears says on his website that one minute per year of age is appropriate, so a two year old gets a two-minute timeout. I personally don't abide by that rule of thumb: mine are longer and more stressful, but the expert advice may work for you. The bell lets the kid know when it's over so you don't have to. The ticking reminds the kid that the timeout is still going on. And the timer itself seems to have some kind of psychic power that causes temporary paralysis in your shrimpy delinquent.

Something I also like to do before the timeout is, make sure the kid understands why he's being punished. I ask the questions "Why do you need a timeout? And what did you just say or do that wasn't nice?" And when it's over, I ask "Why did daddy put you into timeout?" Sometimes they need help with the answers, but most times they don't. They're not stupid—they know what they did.

There are plenty of ways to get through to your kids without hitting. Figure those out and you may avoid building lifelong resentment in your little one.

30. DEVIN, MY LITTLE DEVIL— Every now and then a good smack can bring you back to reality.

"Daddy, I want to smack you in the face." He wasn't smiling.

"You want to what?"

"Smack you in the face." Still no smile.

"You do?"

"Yes."

"Then do it. Go ahead and try it. But I don't think you really want to smack me in the face because that's not a nice thing to do." I stooped down to look him in the eye as I said this, a weak attempt at playing upon his morality.

SMACK!

Then he smiled. And I felt like an idiot. Now I know that attempting to test the moral compass of a child by using reverse psychology may not be such a good idea.

31. MY FAMILY'S COMMUTE— Do what you have to do (sacrifice) and make the best of it.

We all have our stories about the daily grind. We wake up and do what we must to make our lives move along. Luckily for me, I am half of a team. I am in awe of the single parents that take the bus to daycare at the crack of dawn with their child strapped to their chest. You do what you have to do.

I don't usually like to talk about my commute. It exhausts me just thinking about it and most people I know don't believe me when I tell them anyway. But I feel like sharing my family's misery so here it goes in boring detail:

\<begin excerpting\>

5:00 a.m.—Alarm goes off in Queens (two seconds later I slap the snooze button)

5:09 a.m.—Alarm goes off again, my wife and I get out of bed. She heads to the shower, I iron. We don't talk to each other or look at each other until later on in the morning.

6:00 a.m.—Devin gets up to join the party. He turns on "Barney," which makes the morning officially suck, but in a cute way.

6:45 a.m.—We leave the house. All of us are tired and cranky and we act like it.

7:45 a.m.—I drop the wife off at a train station in Brooklyn. We smooch. It tastes like at least one of us forgot to brush.

8:05 a.m.—Devin and I arrive at the front of the preschool; there are no parking spaces on the block. We drive around. Devin insists we are riding the Polar Express.

8:20 a.m.—I find a space. "Are we finished Daddy?" He asks.

8:26 a.m.—I go through the drop-off routine with the boy (and I tell you it's a routine: peeing, hugging, kissing, and convincing him that his day will be fine).

8:45 a.m.—I arrive at the subway station after a three-block walk.

9:30 a.m.—Get off the subway in Manhattan and start looking for coffee. Extra-large, please.

(***Mad, annoyed, tired, stressed, for the next several hours at work. I love non-profit!***)

6:25 p.m.—Meet son, wife, and mother (she works there) at the preschool.

6:35 p.m.—We all pile into the little blue Hyundai.

7:00 p.m.—Drop off mother. Expertly duck the neighbors and extended family.

8:00 p.m.—HOME AGAIN!

<end excerpting>

Sheesh. What a day. I am not even going to get into dinner, bedtime and homework. And the car's *check engine* light is still on.

32. RIDING WITH THE DEVIL— Everything is temporary, and so was this. Patience and parenting pays off.

Sometimes I can't believe that my boy is actually mine, despite the fact that I watched him come into to the world. I have watched him grow up over the last few years to become my doppelganger, my "mini-me." I know darn well he's mine, but sometimes, like the mother in "The Omen," I occasionally have my doubts. Lucky for me, I cut his hair nearly bald over the summer and I did not find the "mark of the beast"—just a big round head like his daddy's.

Anyway, the reason I am going down this path of darkness and woe is because he has the smartest mouth I have ever heard on a child. We have had many successes with my son, although this area is still a challenge. He gets most ornery when he is in the backseat of the car demanding his favorite radio station. Over the last several weeks he has developed an addiction to 1010 WINS news radio. He recites the news stories, knows their catch phrases and taglines by heart, and loves when the news anchors give the time and temperature. However, it starts getting weird when he insists on hearing about the four women found dead in a ditch, or the man that was gunned down in Brooklyn. He doesn't know what the reporters are talking about, but that doesn't stop him from wanting to talk about it himself! When he doesn't get his news, he gets mad. Pissed is probably a more accurate description. "Daddy, I hate you." "Music is stupid." "I don't want to hear this, I want 1010 WINS!" "I don't want to share the radio with you or Mommy." It truly goes on and on. We tell him that what he is saying is not nice and we don't give into his demands when he's being rude, but he never relents.

And, in the interest of making my son a kinder person, neither will I.

33. ANOTHER KID?—Don't go into planned reproduction lightly.

The list of people telling my wife and me that we should give my boy a sibling is growing by the day. One of my own brothers, the oldest, has joined the ranks of folks urging us onto number two.

Me, I'm more of a "why gamble" kind of guy. Caring for one healthy, handsome and grumpy child is challenging enough! Why tempt fate by trying for another? Just as bad, what if I *got* another? You don't need me to tell you that black males have a bad reputation and that raising one is not on the list of easy things to do. The thought of worrying about two kids, much less the possibility of two sons, makes me a bit queasy.

I am the third of four boys so I really understand the difficulties that my parents endured. Besides the fact that they mixed up our names on a daily basis, we put them through four times the number of sick days and flu infections, four open school nights to attend each year, four lunches to pack each morning, chaperoning the same school trips four times, four report cards to review (and dole out praise or discipline for), dozens of outfits to wash and socks to match, four heads to be barbered, etc., etc. I'm overwhelmed just thinking about it.

Keith Devin Morton

And, oh yeah, we ain't got no money. Between me, my wife, and our three college degrees, we'll be paying back loans until we retire in about 60 years. Add to that the day-to-day costs of just living in New York and it's enough to make me think twice about growing the family on a non-profit and social worker salary. Maybe in another few years, my wife and I will discuss it again. Until then, unless I hit the lottery between now and the big one, case closed.

34. KID COMEDY—Just for laughs.

During breakfast one morning, my wife asked our boy to spell her first name. He proudly spelled out "M-O-M-M-Y." After she told him how nicely he spelled "Mommy," she asked him to spell Daddy's name. He smiled that adorable, yet somehow unsettling smile, and giggled the letters, "G-A-Y!" Um, at least he can spell.

35. STOKE THE FLAMES OF WONDERMENT—Appreciate the simple things in life.

When my wife and I took the car to the dealer to once and for all address the check engine light, we had to take the subway to work and preschool.

I take the train every day, but we hadn't taken the boy on the subway in about two years. Not since the early days when my wife would drop me off at the F train station with the boy, a stroller and a prayer for an hour and a half–ride into Manhattan every Thursday and Friday. This stress-inducing memory led me to being totally against commuting with Devin during rush hour in New York City.

My wife, however, ever so gently ("Stop acting like a punk, Keith!") convinced me that it would be fine, and it was. We prepped the boy before we all went underground for our early morning adventure from Queens to Manhattan saying things like, "There will be lots of big people on the train," and, "You'll probably not get a seat kiddo," and, "Stay very close to us." Giving kids a heads up about what they will be experiencing in environments unfamiliar to them tends to be very helpful. They may not understand everything that you are explaining to them, but it's still worth the effort. When we arrived at the underground platform he was in awe, and visibly a bit nervous—but that didn't last long.

"Train tracks just like Thomas's!" he shouted as he struggled to get a closer look. Then, seemingly out of nowhere, the train breezed into the station prompting a smile that spread across his entire cherubic face.

It was priceless.

We stepped onto the train as the family we are and found a place where we could stand together—no seats during rush hour. The doors closed with the familiar "ding dong" signaling that our little journey was set to begin. It's a sound that I remember from my first ride on the subway almost 20 years ago. Once the train was in motion, Devin said (a little too loudly),"Mommy, I like the train." My grinning wife then brought her eyes to mine.

"Great, now people are going to think that we're a bunch of bumpkins that have never been on the subway before." I just adore her sense of humor. We laughed as we were jostled by hard-faced New Yorkers.

As the train moved from station to station, Devin mimicked the whooshing sounds of the brakes, smiling the type of smile that only a three-year-old in a state of pure bliss can. Most adults will never intimately know a child's simplistic happiness ever again. When we got off of the iron horse at Mid-Town Manhattan, we started toward the conductor's post at the center of the train so that Devin could get a glimpse of the real thing (as opposed to Tom Hank's animated character in "The Polar Express"). And we got a good one.

The conductor was in full MTA New York City Transit dress from head to toe, his hat giving him the authentic look that we could have only hoped for. He was an older gentleman with a deep voice and a serious look of duty set deep into his eyes. He was a train man through and through. He would have not looked out of place on any railroad of the last 150 years, aside from the fact that he was black. Sadly the MTA is planning to phase out guys like him and replace them with computer chips and pre-recorded voices. Devin started waving wildly at the man, who was not ashamed of embracing the full-blown train groupie that he is. The conductor nodded politely and mouthed a hello that made my boy's year.

"He looked at me! He looked at me! The conductor looked at me! He said 'hello' to me! Not you, me!" For the rest of the day he talked about his first real experience on the subway. It's amazing how life can produce moments of unexpected joy, even during something as mundane as commuting.

36. BRAVO! BRAVO! (WHAT WAS THAT!?)—Just for laughs.

So I'm in the kitchen, not taking a shot of tequila, when my kid comes up to me in his underwear, a scarf around his neck. He opens the conversation.

"Daddy!"

"What's up kid?"

"I must sing for you!" He's a caroler. Great.

"You do? OK then, sing for me." He clears his throat, or maybe it's a grunt, then he begins his serenade.

"A lease blah dee blah. A lease blah dee blah. A lease blah dee blah [mumble, mumble, mumble] A lease e dah. I wanna wish you a Merry Christmas. I wanna wish you a Merry Christmas. I wanna wish you a Merry Christmas from the bottom of my heart!"

"Wow Devin that was amazing!" I clapped. I hugged. I smiled. It was cute. I thought about teaching him the actual words of the song because people screwing up Christmas songs is one of my pet peeves. Then I thought better of it.

37. TIPPING TIME!—Tip as much as you can even if it hurts (and it will hurt).

Tipping is something that you should take seriously, especially when it comes to your child's caregivers. Even if your child's caregiver is your mother you should get her a special gift for all that she does. At the end of the day, it's the thought that counts

As a broke, disgruntled non-profit employee I get depressed/stressed holiday time. Why you ask? Tipping and gift-giving. For the most part I can ignore family; however the people I can't ignore are the staff at the preschool. How much do you give the person that takes care of your most prized possession, your kid, all day long? Nothing ever seems to be enough. My wife tips the parking lot attendant $1-$2 a day just for parking and fetching Dimples (a.k.a. the Hyundai). The teachers, on the other hand, care for my cursing, poop-covered, rowdy, and adorable child for nine hours a day—he's my offspring and I wouldn't want that job! Do they get gifts, cash, cookies, movie tickets, all of the above, or something else entirely?

Gift cards seem to be the most popular option these days. They are quick and easy and require very little thought or effort. They are literally a thoughtless gift! That may sound bad on the surface but in reality it's a fantastic plus. The cards gives the recipient flexibility in choosing their own gift instead of whatever lousy useless thing you could come up with on your own. You also have the choice of directing the purchase to a store by buying a store-specific card, or the really lazy debit card version that can be used anywhere. The only challenge with gift cards is determining the denomination. Many businesses and schools have a maximum limit on the monetary value of the gifts employees can accept so you can check those guidelines. If no guidelines exist then give what you can—teachers and other caregivers know that most working people aren't rich and will gladly accept your gift. It is the thought that counts after all. Right?

38. THE SHOWS—Go to as many of your child's shows, performances, and other events as you can tolerate.

I leave work early every time my son has a show. Once I know the date of a show, whether it's for Halloween or Christmas, I tell my boss that I'm going to need a half-day. Giving a lot of notice tends to make it easier. Once in a while bosses, mostly those without lives or kids, will be jerks about it and might not give you the time off you ask for, but you'll never know unless you ask.

Christmastime in preschool means holiday parties and, unfortunately, holiday shows. It's a rite of passage to participate in a so-lame-its-cute school show at some point in your childhood. In our heads, we knew that nothing good could come from a show in which my boy was expected to perform. But in our hearts, we hoped for the best. The week before the show, we tried to mentally prepare the little grouch for his small stage debut.

"Devin, we can't wait to see you sing and dance at the holiday show."

"Devin, on Thursday Mommy and Daddy will watch you perform all the great songs you've learned."

"Devin, we can't wait to see you sing and dance!"

Etc., etc. We thought he was ready.

My wife and I were on holiday break from work the week leading up to the show. It was a bitterly cold week that begged us to stay in the house and forget trekking out into the world. Forget the show. Forgo the long ride into Brooklyn. Our son was three at the time, hardly old enough to resent us down the road for not forcing him to sing in a Christmas show. But our desire to see the cuteness of 20 kids carry us into the holiday was too strong to resist. We were going to the show and mommy bought Devin a special sweater just for the occasion.

We figured we'd bring him in late just for his performance in the afternoon. Why send him to school early when he could just sit at home with his parents until show time? I actually asked the teacher if this was a good idea and she said it was fine. Big mistake. We walked in at 3:30 to find all the kids seated and ready to start the show. For some reason, my son is kind of popular and whenever he enters his class, he's greeted like Norm from "Cheers" by his classmates ("Devin!"). This time it was his toddler bar buddies and their assorted parents.

Devin fell into his usual "I hate you all" mode and acted like he didn't want to be there. Perhaps he really didn't. He folded his fingers into fists, furrowed his brow and stopped in his tracks. Not wanting to make a scene, we thought about leaving him where he stood. Only his favorite teacher was able to coax him into his chair on the makeshift stage with the others.

Once my boy took his place, he folded his arms and scowled at the crowd. The show started. The scowling continued. The kids sang (or at least the ones not picking their noses, staring blankly at the ceiling, or crying), and he kept busy by scowling. Scowling. Still scowling. More scowling. And even more scowling. Then the kids started a holiday train of some kind with a dab of hip shaking, which made the boy crack a smile. He's ALIVE! And he was joining the love train. He sang the last three or four songs and even managed to look like he was having fun. Its stories like this (and just about every other in this book) that we'll use to embarrass him when he gets older.

Going to as many school functions as possible brings you much closer to your family. These are the things that you'll remember about your kid when they are running their own business or signing autographs someday. The whole "family man" thing can be bizarre, but I wouldn't miss it for anything.

39. IS THIS THE REMIX?—Are they really still singing these songs? We should sing more Bob Marley in school.

"Jimmy red car and I don't care.
Jimmy red car and I don't care.
Jimmy red care and I don't caaaaaaaaaaaare!
My monster's run away."

As much as I hate the original "Jimmy Crack Corn" in its historical minstrel context, I kind of like my son's remix. It must be fun being a snot-nosed, cookie munching, song mangling three-year-old. At least he's not singing Dixie, which was written around the same time as "Jimmy Crack Corn" and opens "Oh I wish I was in the land of cotton, Old times there are not forgotten…" Need I say more? Yes many people say it's a southern pride song, not a racist song, and I can accept how that may be true. But I don't like it. "Three Little Birds" by the reggae master Bob Marley seems a much better option.

40. THAT'S THE FEVER TALKING—Another funny conversation that wasn't funny at the time.

"Oh, the poor baby has a fever!" I said to the Devil when I picked him up early from preschool, following a call from the school administrator.

"No I don't." He replied.

"Yes you do. And you're going to need a little medicine, too, when we get home."

"No I don't."

"How do you feel?"

"Good."

"You're sick, little guy."

"No I'm not, so shut your stinky mouth."

He just couldn't admit it, the little disrespectful thing. Later, at home,

"Vin, stop jumping up and down on the bed, you're sick and you need to rest."

"I'm not sick!"

"Yes, you are."

"No I'm not."

Then he sat down on the bed and reluctantly laid his head on his pillow.

"What's wrong?" I ask.

Keith Devin Morton

"I don't feel well."

"That's because you're jumping up and down on your bed with a fever when you should be resting."

"Shut up, Daddy."

41. MY KID IS SMARTER THAN YOURS—Don't get cocky, your child doesn't walk on water.

Always be your child's biggest cheerleader. Who will stand up for your kid, if not you? If parents had licenses, the infraction for not doing so would mean five points off of yours. However, be reasonable in your expectations and don't cheer so loud that other parents want to hit you with their car.

My kid is smarter than yours. OK, that may not be true, but don't we all like to think that about our offspring? It's kind of like having a kid that's not all that cute and thinking he or she is the next Denzel or Halle. We, as parents, are blind to the reality that our children might possibly have average looks and IQs. And, for the most part, I'd have it no other way. It's our love of our kids that allows us to see the beauty and potential in them long before they even know they possess it. Long before *anyone* knows, for that matter.

Of course we can also have the opposite effect and crush an otherwise normal kid with harsh words and loveless criticism. We must consciously avoid being that kind of parent at all costs.

We have to be honest with ourselves. There are going to be some things that our kids will not be good at or be interested in. You may *want* a basketball champion deep down in your loins when what you *have* is the tetherball master. Or in the future, you may want your kid to be a concert pianist when all they can or want to do is blow "Mary Had a Little Lamb" on their kazoo.

Then there are times when parents need to adjust to their children's changing abilities. For example, some kids are as smart as the day is long for the first several years of their lives, learning everything until they plateau. It's a real phenomenon that I learned about from a seasoned educator.

It's safe to assume that potential can, and will, manifest itself in your child, but it may not be in the form that you were expecting.

I started thinking about all this stuff after a conversation with my boss, a career educator who is the head of a department that serves thousands of kids with a variety of interests. Her advice to me was to remember that a well-rounded child should be the goal. This means that it's great if your kid can read and count, but now it's time to work on comprehension, writing, fine motor skills, arts and music, geography, and one thousand other things. Dads (and Moms), we sure do have a long way to go!

42. CAREER MENTORS—Find a mentor to help advance, or at least support, your career.

     I never understood the value of a mentor until I had one of my own. As a father, having a professional relationship with someone that can help you make the right career decisions gives you a peace of mind. Also, fatherhood is stressful enough, so having a support system at the office can add to stability in your home life.

     I am a constant ball of anxiety. About three years ago, I was even more stressed. I had a new baby, a new college degree, and an old, depressing job. After being the administrative manager of a mental health clinic for five years, I was ready for a change. I *needed* a change. So I stopped sending my resume to uninteresting places where my only hope was to get an interview, and instead started to send my resume to places where I thought I might actually like to work. I came across a job posting for an operations manager (whatever that was) at a children's center in Manhattan and I thought, "I like kids, I guess." I sent in my resume.

     Getting the call for an interview was a shock. In my head I had convinced myself that I was a clinic guy, not a children's center guy. I was getting job offers to work in hospitals and clinics, and bullet point by bullet point, my resume said that was the type of career I should pursue. Yet, someone out there in the abyss that is job-seeking saw my resume for the skill, not the industry. Finally, some luck! I went on the interview and the first face I saw belonged to someone that looked like me, which relaxed me—but only for a second. Upon further observation, I realized that all the kids and parents and staff were white. Toto, we're not in Manhattan anymore—I was in Kansas! Sweat beaded on my forehead, advertising my discomfort. Then I met Catherine, the director of the center, and I was at ease again. Not because she looked like me (far from it), but because I could immediately sense her genuineness. After speaking to her for about an hour I knew I wanted to work with her, despite the fact that I thought the environment was a teensy bit outside of my comfort zone.

I got the job and that's when my real career began. It was there that I learned how to manage budgets, supervised the largest staff I've ever had, and discovered that my brain could work through some complex organizational crap. And with me the whole time, rooting me on, supporting me, challenging me, and listening to my occasional diatribes was Catherine. She became my career mentor, my sponsor, and my friend. To this day we openly and honestly talk about race issues and life issues and when she can't relate she doesn't act like she can, and she doesn't try to BS me with fakeness.

When Catherine was promoted, she encouraged me to throw my hat and resume into the ring for an internal promotion. The position was a challenging one and I wasn't convinced that I could do it (the person that held the job before me was a Harvard MBA), but she insisted that I could. Without people like Catherine in your corner, many hardworking folk like me, black men to be more specific, find it much harder to be noticed. Experts say that most career success comes from the relationships we make, and I'm proof of that being true. Being able to boast a decent, albeit low-paying job, makes raising a child just a little easier.

I started thinking about my friend and her influence on my career only after she resigned from her position to pursue a challenging new opportunity. She's left me to carry on without her. Alone. The dynamic duo became the dynamic *uno*. At first I wished her to the cornfield as the evil kids in "Children of the Corn" did to their parents, but I knew that was unfair. It was selfish. Eventually, I understood that life would go on and that the support she had given me and the lessons I learned from her would live no matter what position she held in the world. She had left me with more tools that I would be able to use going forward. That's what a good mentor does.

43. LOVE—Create your own definition of what love is and you won't be off the mark.

After a few days of searching my quirky soul, I believe that I discovered what love means to me. I've single-handedly developed criteria for measuring and quantifying love. The theory is based on my being a dad, and the unconditional love of a parent for a child. Nevertheless, it's transferable to all relationships. Needless to say, I am a genius. Here is what I determined love between humans is:

1. When you can hold another person's disgusting poopy diaper in the palm of your left hand, and wipe their butt with your right, without any hopes of salary.

2. When you can hold another person in your arms and allow them to cough, sneeze, bleed, or throw up on you without caring about contracting something.

3. When you truly want to see a person find success and be happy without even the slightest hint of jealousy or envy. (This is a hard one because many jealous folk have no clue that they are jealous.)

4. When you would do anything, including risk your own life, to see a person not suffer mentally or physically, fail, or endure hardship.

5. When in conversation you find yourself actually listening to a person with a deep, sincere interest be-

cause you care about what they have to say, rather than thinking about all the witty things you want to say in response.

Now, think about all the people that you'd do *all* of the above for. Those are the people that you love so much that that you often find yourself stressing about their wellbeing; you think about their happiness more than your own. More than likely, if you have children, they are the ones. You are not a martyr when it comes to these people, you just love them. Some people think that this love is unhealthy, and they may be right, though it doesn't matter much.

Now think about the people that you'd do four out of five of the things for, three out of five, and so on. That's when you uncover varying degrees of love. The first tier, generally speaking, is reserved for your kids, your spouse, and maybe your parents. The second tier for your closest friends and relatives. And so on and so forth.

The next time you're hanging with the homies or laughing with your cousins at a family gathering, think about the people in the room, and HONESTLY ask yourself, "Whose ass would I wipe?" The answer to that question will probably astound you.

Love, peace, and Charmin.

44. TIMEOUTS—Discipline can be very challenging, even for the best parents.

Too many people have criticized me for advocating non-corporal punishments as a means of discipline. They talk about the good ol' days when our parents beat the crap out of us at the drop of a hat. All I have to say to that is that my father whooped me, and these days we don't talk much (twice last year for about 20 minutes in total). I got smacked around on more than one occasion, which to me is the point—knowing a beating was imminent never prevented me from doing the bad stuff I always found myself doing. Think about it: After your first-ever beating did you stop misbehaving, or do you recall getting spanked more than once? If it was more than once, then how effective was the beating? How many times did you say to yourself, "If I do 'X,' then my mother/father is going to kick my ass," and then you did "X" anyway? Think about it.

That's not to say that non-corporal punishments are easy. I would argue that the most challenging thing about parenting a small child is discipline. Being consistent is hard, ranking offenses based on severity is almost impossible, and getting the outcome you want is never guaranteed.

Keith Devin Morton

Trying to discipline my little terror can be a challenge. To Devin, timeout is the equivalent of waterboarding (does that make me Dick Cheney? Yikes.), or someone deciding to destroy all the chicken nuggets in the world. Personally, I *wish* someone would put me in a corner and tell me not to come out until I'm told to—I'd take the naughty step before a spanking any day. But, alas, a three-year-old has no way of understanding the value of meditation time. Therefore, my wife and I are left with the task of dragging a flailing, crying, bundle of crazy to his non-physical punishment. Here's how the last incident went down between the wife and Devin:

"You're hitting? I think you need a timeout."

"Nooooooooooooooo! I don't want a timeout!"

"Well you need one because you were hitting. Let's go."

"Nooooooooooooooo! I don't want to! I hate you, Mommy!"

"That's not nice, Devin. Now, sit down and shut your mouth."

By this point the super-sized tears are flowing and the fake coughing has started. My wife walks away after setting the egg timer. The coughing continues and the tears flow like rivers. The coughing is a warning sign. We know our boy well enough to understand that it can get really ugly when he's upset and the coughing begins. I look at the wife, she looks at me, and then on cue, the Devil pukes. Yes, when he gets riled up, he throws up. It's one of the nastiest defense mechanisms I've ever known. This time we were lucky because he caught the mess in his hand, and it wasn't too much.

Other times we are not so lucky and we end up changing sheets or scrubbing carpet.

The problem is that you never feel like you got your point across when, in the middle of disciplining your kid, you stop to clean up puke. It's like you lost a battle that you were sure you were going to win. I've been told to make him clean it up; though I think an uncoordinated little boy being forced to clean up vomit through the tears is cruel and unusual. Kids still need to feel loved, even when Mommy and Daddy are in discipline mode. A fiercely upset child is difficult to manage without turning it into a battle of wills. I've resigned myself to the fact that parenting can sometimes be disgusting.

Had we opted for the beating odds are that he still would have been crying hard enough to throw up and he may have been scared or physically hurt. Spankings, the parental version of shock and awe, have approximately the same effectiveness if used as a form of disciplining kids: temporary with the potential of ongoing lingering resentment, or just plain sadness and unhealthy fear.

45. GETAWAYS—Get away from the kids to preserve your remaining sanity, even if only for one night.

Whenever my wife and I can't figure out what we want to do on a special occasion, the most recent being our fourth wedding anniversary, we go to a casino. I know this is wrong. Fortunately, we're the world's worst gamblers so we only play the slots. We also set a low budget for the amount of money we can part with. I had a room comp that was burning a hole in my pocket, so we dropped off the kid at Great Grandma's house, rented a Mazda 6, and zoom zoomed to Atlantic City, New Jersey.

As expected, we didn't win a thing, though we felt like winners all night. Why you wonder? Because Devin was 130 miles away. There is nothing quite like a night away from the horrors joys of parenting. We don't run away often, maybe once or twice a year, and it's amazing. We do adult things, we do childish things, we do geriatric things, and we do them all without our take-along audience. It's the kind of fun that only a parent can understand.

Now that I'm officially in my *late* twenties (and a month away from 30 as of this writing), a parent, and smack in the middle of family life, I can appreciate the joys of an overnight with the wife. Knowing that someone, other than me, is out in the world getting cursed out by the boy as I toss back a shot of tequila makes for a smooth drink. Understanding that I will likely not have filet mignon again the rest of this year (and that it will take me about as long to pay off the meal) is priceless.

I may have lost $140 at the slots, but I won a teeny bit of sanity. Trust me folks, taking a few nights off does wonders for your mind, your marriage, and your family during the other 362 days a year. Taking a breather on a regular basis is a must. If you don't take care of your needs every now and again then how can you take care of others? You have to put back the energy that you expend tending to others and a good way to do that is taking time for yourself.

46. BEING THE ALPHA DUDE— Be protective, not stupid.

As it was, I wasn't having the best day ever. My mother had called to inform me that the director of my son's school, where my mother also works, wanted to talk to me about my child's future and how to help him adjust. She mentioned some "free services" that might be helpful. I've been in the early childhood education business for the last three years and I'll tell you right now that I do not look forward to a meeting about my kid's inability to adjust. Or free services. Not fun at all. Then the wife insisted on dragging me to the mall.

We walked in through the Macy's entrance because it was closest to the car, and after taking about two steps, a t-shirt clad twenty-something took my wife by the elbow and started to lay his lines down. I was a few feet behind my lady holding Devin's hand, when I felt my lip curl. The Mack's friend watched on smiling, my wife said nothing, though I did.

"Don't touch my wife, man."

In hindsight it was a lame line, but it felt manly as hell at the time, deep and authoritative. When I realized I might have to argue or fight after my instinct to stand up to the disrespectful young men had already put me out there, I braced for what might come next. What I got surprised, and relieved me.

"Oh, my bad man," the Mack said with a guilty/embarrassed grin.

That was it. Fiercer words have slipped from my lips in the past while playing the role of alpha male in defense of my wife. When I look back at the times in my life when being a man was more important to me than being a *smart* man, I wonder how I made it this far. I'm glad that my corny one-liner was not the one to finally do me in (though I fight like a rabid squirrel and could have taken those guys).

Devin, in typical kid fashion, didn't even bat an eyelash at the exchange. His focus was on chicken nuggets, and all he knew was that those guys didn't have any.

47. THIS IS NOT AN EMERGENCY—Another funny moment with a serious point.

"Daddy, come on and play with me." My son beckoned me to his train set in earnest.

"OK, as soon as I finish reading this article."

"Daaaaaaaaaaddy, I need you to play with me."

"Just a minute, OK?" I continued reading the article, looking up from my magazine only after I heard Devin pick up the phone. I got a glimpse of him dialing three numbers.

"What are you doing?! Hang up the phone now!" My boy looked at me with rebellion in his eyes.

"I'm calling the police on you to take you to jail because you won't play with me."

"Hang it up," I said icily. Finally he hung up the phone. I wanted to tell him that you never call the police on a black man unless he's doing something really, really horrible. Instead, I opted for a less political statement.

"Devin, you should only call 911 when there is an emergency, like if Mommy or Daddy is hurt."

"I'm not talking to you anymore, Daddy." He walked away.

48. DECISION MAKING—Learn to live with the consequences of your choices.

The proverbial shit hit the fan when I got a call at my job from the Devil's school. He was losing his damn mind in the background as I talked to a supervisor. I don't know the details, but apparently someone asked him to do something that he didn't want to do and it ended with him throwing a bunch of toys onto the floor, pissing off his classmates who put them away neatly, and panicking the staff. The kid can be intense—even I can't deny that.

The incident, the most recent of several, made us finally confront a decision that we just couldn't make until this point. After consulting with several child development professionals, we came to the conclusion that Devin needs shorter days. My wife resigned from her position, taking a lower-paying, part-time, unionized job with full benefits. Meanwhile, I asked my boss for shorter work days until the wife started her new job, so I could pick my boy up from school earlier.

Had you told me four years ago that my wife and I would be making these kinds of sacrifices; I'd have called you stupid. But here we are doing just that. I could have never predicted my boy's personality and disposition—not in a million years. I love that little boy more than ANYTHING on this planet, despite the fact that he is the meanest, grouchiest, most stubborn person I've ever known (myself not included). But I'm not backing down. This kid has a daddy and mommy who are in it for the long haul and he had better recognize!

The overall outcome of our schedule adjustment was ASTOUNDING. The boy blossomed in school, reclaiming his exceptional academic standing amongst little people. For months before the change, we had been getting regular incident reports. After five weeks on Devin's shortened schedule, we didn't get a single report of bad behavior—not just in school, but at home, too. He became more relaxed, it was easier to get him into bed at night, and he started trying new foods—all things that we thought would never be possible. He became an all-around pleasant kid, reminding us that there are some real joys associated with parenting.

I'm humbled by the experience because I know that many parents would love to be able to do what we are doing. For thousands of reasons (many being financial, some being emotional) they cannot. I understand that and I will not allow myself to take this gift for granted. The truth is that we are suffering financially on many fronts, though we believe this to be temporary, which makes it worth it.

49. SMOOCHES FROM THE DEVIL—Enjoy the kisses now, they will not last forever.

Showing and receiving affection from our kids can be a difficult thing. Many of us do not remember the last time we gave our dad a kiss, especially us guys. For the most part we stopped kissing daddy around the time we started kissing girls. It's a natural progression. Keep that in mind the next time your child gives you a smooch. Soon they may be gone for good.

Until recently my boy could not give a memorable kiss on the cheek. He was terrible. It was like planting a lifeless mackerel from the local fish market on your cheek. The kid was a mess. No suction. His mother and I have smooched the boy quite a bit in the last three (almost four) years and for some reason he was not learning from our example. Then one night before bed he told me he wanted to give me a kiss goodnight. He planted one right on the meaty part of my cheek and I cracked up because it was an actual smooch, sound effects and all.

He knew that he had learned a neat trick because that night he volunteered to give me the kiss instead of me begging him to show his daddy some love. Just one of those moments in parenting that reminds you that life could be much worse. Still, I'd like to know where

Keith Devin Morton

he suddenly learned that a kiss was not just lips pressed against a cheek. Am I going to have to talk to some little girl's parents before his fourth birthday?

50. POTTY TRAINED—Get prepared for the challenges associated with potty training.

A potty-trained child is a beautiful thing. It saves money and is more sanitary—at least until you find yourself holding a 40-pound kid over a poop-covered toilet in a public bathroom. It's those instances when you are out and about in the city and your kid has to go to the bathroom that you find yourself wishing that you could put your potty-trained kid in a diaper.

My boy was a late bloomer when it came to potty training. Maybe that's why only recently have I started to notice that most men's restrooms are stupid. The urinals are too high for the average five-year old to walk up to and do his business, much less a three or four year old. They are also often covered in urine, as is the floor directly beneath them. The toilet stalls are even worse because let's face it: No one goes #2 in public unless it's urgent. If it's not urgent, you'll wait until you're home, or some other place that is more private and conducive to reading. And for some strange reason after an urgent public poop, most men lose hand function, leaving them unable to flush. So what does all that mean for us dads with small children? Children, mind you, who have no way of understanding that a toilet seat is like a gi-

Keith Devin Morton

ant uncovered petri dish? It means that you had better renew your gym membership and pay special attention to strengthening your bicep and forearm muscles.

51. PEEING—We have to teach them EVERYTHING!

Once Devin started potty-training, it dawned on my wife that living with guys is nothing like living with ladies. She lived with her mother and sister for most of her life and had no clue what it would be like to live in an apartment outnumbered by dudes. Now as our boy grows, she's starting to see what she's in for. We pick our noses, fart and laugh about it, belch and try to make the other guy smell it, and are generally amused by our pudgy bellies. My wife joins in on occasion, commenting on stinky breath and smelly feet in her playful way, but aside from that it's a house of testosterone. Shalawn can deal pretty well with most of the boy stuff, except for one thing: bad aim.

I was well into my teens before I cared about my aim, so I let the wife know that she had a long way to go before the toilet seat would be regularly dry. I lived with three brothers, so I learned quickly to not plop down onto the toilet without running a few sheets of TP over it (assuming there was any on the roll). My mother understood the rules too, but she sometimes forgot. And we all knew when she failed to follow the unspoken rules of living with boys because she would yell out "who peed all over the toilet seat?" or "I fell in!"

Keith Devin Morton

Now it's Devin's mother's turn to enjoy raising a boy—and, being Devin, he's a little bit of a special case. We've had some bizarre late night encounters with the boy. He's really good at getting up at night and going to the bathroom. Nine out of 10 times he goes without incident, which is awesome.

Then there's the one in ten.

We have watched him walk into the hall, turn around go back into his bedroom, then pee on his pillow while standing alongside his bed—all with his eyes closed. We've had to redirect him and send him to the bathroom because he was so confused and tired. We've dragged him out of the kitchen for the same reason. But the real issue is that in the bathroom, whether he's sleep-walking or wide awake, he pees everywhere. We have a rug that we may have to burn. As a father, and a former offender, I have promised to work on aim with my son. It's the least I can do.

I've heard that dropping a few Cheerios (a toddler/preschool staple) into the toilet and challenging your little one to aim for them works well. It may not be feasible to run into the bathroom each time your child does to add food to the toilet, but I can see keeping a small bag next to the commode and encouraging the boys to drop in two or three before they go. It's worth a shot. I'll go with patience and constant reminders, which just seem easier.

52. "THE BIG C" AND ME— Prevent disease whenever possible.

It's important to know if you have a family history of disease. Those who know are ahead of the game when it comes to prevention because we can ask the doc to keep an eye out for signs during our annual checkup. Sadly, too many of us don't know one of the essential people that could tell you what your hereditary risks are: dad. This shouldn't stop you from asking your doctor questions, requesting various detection tests and asking the family that you do know about illnesses that they have dealt with.

A couple of years ago I had my first colonoscopy. No it's not typical for a guy in his mid-twenties to have the marginally disturbing anal-probing procedure, but I did. There were two major reasons for me to get my young colon checked out: one was my family and the other was my family history.

During a routine wellness visit with my doctor, the greatest internist I've ever had the pleasure of knowing, we started to revisit my family history of disease. I reminded him of the diabetes, the high blood pressure, and the thyroid conditions. He took notes and blood (at the time he still took blood himself, though he has "people" that do it now). I then opened up about my family history in regards to colon cancer. He asked me if anyone in my immediate family had the disease. I told him yes. He asked me who they were and their ages, I told him that too. He looked at me and smiled. He said, "You need to have a colonoscopy." I replied that yes I was in a high-risk category (me being a black male and all), but not quite 50 years old yet, which is the standard age for people to start getting checked. Then he explained something to me that I had never heard before.

If there is a strong family history of colon cancer where an immediate family member, (your father, mother, or sibling) has or has had the disease, then you should have a colonoscopy ten years earlier than whatever the age of the youngest person with the disease was at the time of their diagnosis.

Crap. I needed a colonoscopy. I set up an appointment with one of the most well-regarded specialists in NYC, who explained that it usually takes about ten years for a polyp to become cancer, which is why colon cancer is one of the more preventable and treatable cancers. If you have the procedure done around the time when you may start forming polyps, you can have any polyps they find removed and substantially reduce your chances of developing the disease.

But it wasn't that detailed explanation that inspired me to take laxatives and have a camera shoved up my butt. As far as I was concerned, I had a wife and a kid to take care of, so I was getting the recommended colonoscopy. On the bright side the drugs for the procedure are friggin' awesome and all I remember is asking the doctor if he was going to buy me a drink before sticking that thing up my ass, and then I was out. I woke up in recovery feeling good about life. A nurse handed me a picture of my insides, told me that a polyp was removed and would be biopsied, and a couple of weeks later I was given a clean bill, and told that I would need to have it done all over again at 30.

The moral of the story is to get regular checkups, know your family history, report it clearly to your doctor, and take action. Do it for yourself and do it for your family. Live long and prosper, dammit—life is too short not to.

53. PROMOTE GOOD HYGEINE—No one likes a stinky kid. Or a stinky adult, for that matter.

Ever try convincing a kid that his hands are dirty when he doesn't see anything? The problem with germs is that with kids, seeing is believing. You're better off trying to teach habits, not the reasoning behind them. Getting your child to brush her teeth everyday will be much easier than convincing them that their teeth will fall out if they don't.

Of the 413 times a day that my son uses the restroom, he probably washes his hands about four. When I catch him, I make sure that he washes thoroughly with soap (I really have to sell the soap part). Then there's me, who washes his hands 413 times a day out of sheer paranoia about contracting communicable illnesses.

While I have patience for little boys with germy hands, I have absolutely no tolerance for adult males. My hunch is that men don't feel the need to wash their hands after they urinate because they hold onto a belief that touching their "member" is like touching their arm, or more sadly, their finger. After all no one washes their hands every time they pat their biceps and welcome their lady friends to the gun show. Men psychologically equate the two acts, which is obviously nasty. How many times have you seen a man publicly walk away from a urinal, or a stall and then right out the door? Probably every disgusting day. Heck, you may be that dude.

I know that my boy is always in a rush and 40 seconds of hand washing seems cumbersome, so I've been trying to get him to do an anti-bacterial hand gel pump (thanks to Mom for keeping us stocked) after every #1 and an elbow-to-fingertips washing after every #2. It kind of works, though I'm still a big fan of soap and water after every time you walk into a bathroom whether you go or not.

In general kids have good memories and choose not to wash their hands more because they don't want to be bothered than because they forgot. Constantly telling them to wash their hands and brush their teeth and bathe lets children know that those things are important. Eventually they'll believe you. In the meantime make it fun and get the cartoon character or crayon inspired toothbrush, the soap dispenser shaped like an animal (or whatever rocks your kid's world) and a fun washcloth/towel set.

54. VISIT THE DENTIST—Get to the dentist well before the first cavity.

Dental hygiene is serious business. Brushing and flossing are lifelong habits that need to start when you are very young. Going to the dentist twice a year is also crucial to good oral health. You don't want your mouth to be the home of 16 fillings and three crowns all before 30 like someone I know!

Going to the dentist can be a harrowing experience for rational adults, so imagine what it could be like for a four year old. At the dentist's office, kids find themselves face to face with big, serious-looking chairs, strange metal instruments that look more like they belong in Daddy's tool box, gurgling suction devices, weird whirring spittoons, and a spotlight lamp that blinds you as if you're under interrogation. Then, some strange lady in a mask pries your mouth open with her latex-gloved fingers to (allegedly) count your teeth. It could be horrible, unless you are prepared.

In preparation for Devin's first-ever visit to the dentist, my wife told him exactly what to expect—from the X-ray to the free toothbrush. The result was a mostly-relaxed kid sitting in the dentist's chair (though he almost lost it when the big scary dentist first walked into the room, despite her Winnie the Pooh scrubs and sincere smile). He giggled when he spit into the suction funnel and got a kick out of having his already gleaming teeth polished. It was even fun for the wife and me because we were able to see the big boy molars that are coming in and were shown the proper way to floss Devin's hard-to-reach teeth.

Take advantage of the early dental appointments. Devin has no fear of the dentist because his first visit was such a pleasant one. He'll be going every six months from here on out. Strangely, lots of parents have the idea that the first set of teeth is not very important because they'll all come out anyway, which is a flawed theory. A life of good dental hygiene begins with the first set. I try to think of them as the starter set, kind of like buying a 3-series BMW then moving up to the 7. Plus it's important to make sure that everything in your child's mouth is developing normally.

Had I, through no fault of my own, not missed over 10 years of dental visits (mostly because of no health insurance and no money), I might not be sitting at my computer right now with a decomposing filling and a tooth in need of a root canal. Heck, I have so much new hardware in my mouth that some people would call my teeth bionic. Just go to the dentist, make sure your kid goes, and stop being a chicken.

55. DREAMS CHANGE— Nurture their dreams from the beginning and they'll never have regrets.

Kids start dreaming young. They talk about driving cars and being able to stay up late when they are older. They even talk about the work they want to do for a living when they are old enough to work. If you feel compelled to tell your child that they can't be a race car driver when they grow up because you want them to go to medical school, get over it. It's safe to assume that most people don't hold onto their preschool career goals. I once knew a girl that wanted to be a mermaid when she grew up. We can all guess how that turned out.

My son has declared himself our housekeeper. After getting over the initial shock, we couldn't be more thrilled. We feel very Upper East Side now, and it's all thanks to the boy. Sure, he's four, but he is totally committed to being the best darn housekeeper we've ever had. The best part is that we only have to pay him in chicken nuggets, quarters, and love. I know that some of you are wondering how my wife and I have arrived at such great fortune. Well, it all started one morning:

"Daddy. Daddy. Daddy."

"What kid?" I asked through the foam of minty fresh toothpaste.

"I'm the housekeeper," he grinned.

"Huh? I thought you were the bus driver."

"I am. I work for the Manhattan Division, but I'm also the housekeeper." We have a mini Tony Danza here. And without question he's the boss. Great.

Moments later we decided to use some psychological warfare to deter the boy from his newly chosen profession. (I really want him to be a scientist of some kind.) We commenced the interrogation.

"Do you know what a housekeeper does?"

"Uh, no."

"Well a housekeeper has to do all the cooking and cleaning for a family. That means when you get home from school you'll have to clean the bedrooms, the bathroom, and the kitchen. Then once all that is done, you'll have to cook us dinner. Do you still want the job?"

"Yes. When I get home from school I'm going to clean the whole house and cook dinner."

"So what are you cooking tonight, kid?"

"Hot dogs and broccoli for you, me, and Mommy."

That evening, I left my office feeling the weight of another long day, and that of the commute ahead, in every stride. I pulled my cellular from my pocket and called home.

"Hey. What are you guys doing?"

"Devin's cleaning up. He was set in his mind that he was the housekeeper and that he had work to do. It was all he could talk about until he got into the house and got to work."

Not Superdad

I picked up the pace, cutting through the thick city crowds faster than my shoes knew how. I had to catch my reformed Devil in action. I knew it was not likely, my commute being 90 minutes and all, but I tried anyway. By the time I reached home the boy was in bed. But my arrival gave him an excuse to run from his bedroom and greet me. Between him and his mother I found out that Devin won a sticker in school because of his great singing, that he cleaned up his bedroom, put away his clean laundry, picked up some clothes in my room, and wiped down the bathroom sink and kitchen table. He even swept a little and made the salad we had with dinner.

His pride beamed from his face. For all his hard work he earned fifty cents and a lollipop. With ongoing encouragement and suitable rewards a child can feel like he's part of something bigger and not just a cog in the family wheel, I know that now. Unfortunately after a few days the energy fizzled and we let it.

56. CREATIVE PARENTING— Don't be afraid to use unorthodox parenting techniques.

Unorthodox parenting is fine, as long as you exercise common sense. Don't do anything that will endanger you or your child, and pull out the crazy ideas when it's essential, not just convenient.

This entry is a big shout-out to my wife for one of her displays of darn good parenting:

When I returned home one night after running some errands, my wife was telling the boy that it was 7:00 and that he had 30 minutes until bedtime. My son's bedtime is law, seven days a week, and he takes it as such. Seven o'clock is when you start to wind down and get ready for bed. And when the big hand is on the six and the little one is on the seven you are under the covers. What he didn't know was that it was actually 6:00. After putting the boy in the shower, the wife had seized her opportunity and moved all the clocks in the apartment ahead one hour.

I was a little disoriented at first. Then I was utterly impressed. My wife had manipulated time! Then she simply said, "He's been fussing and carrying on all day. He needs to go to bed. I can't take it anymore." I don't care what anyone says, that was awesome. The boy was snoring by 6:33. We had the whole rest of the night to relax.

57. VOLUNTEERING—Building charity into a child's everyday life is a beautiful thing.

I'll admit that I'm not the biggest fan of volunteering, although I believe it to be essential for the success of any civilized society. It's not really the volunteering that makes me skittish, but the volunteers themselves. In my work at a non-profit, I've come across many volunteers that feel forced into service by their bosses, their companies, or the need to improve upon their college applications. The personal time that I have donated to a cause has been done as an adult with a true passion for the work I was doing, not because I felt coerced.

Passion for the cause is the key to any successful volunteer project—volunteering should never feel like drudgery. If you volunteer for a community project and you start fantasizing about the hum of a dental drill as it descends on your cavity, then you have volunteered for the wrong assignment. If you are suffering, the project will suffer along with you. Its passion and a true commitment that make you want to do a good job. Remember though, that a bad job is a bad job whether you are a paid laborer or a volunteer—you cannot justify doing a lousy job because you are doing it out of the kindness of your heart. That's why any volunteer project that you undertake should be something you care about and can give one hundred percent to.

When your children see you dedicated to a cause, movement, or project that is bigger than you, and deeply important to you, your commitment will be clear to them and they'll want that for themselves. Small children can sense strong positive feelings; they know when you are satisfied and fulfilled. And when they can't sense it, you can simply tell them. Explain how you helped clean out a vacant lot and how you plan on helping to turn it into a community garden. Tell them how you helped paint a community center. Let them know that you are mentoring a teenager and that you hope to help him get into college. Hearing these kinds of stories, even if you are telling them to the ears of a three-year-old, will surely have an impact on them and their futures. Kids know the joy of accomplishment and if you pass that feeling along to them with humility and wisdom, they will be better people because of it.

As busy fathers with jobs and responsibilities we can easily make the excuse that we are too busy to give of our time. I understand that sentiment very well. I rush around one of the largest cities in the U.S. every single day from home to preschool to my office, back to pre-school, off to the supermarket, back home. In between, there is laundry that needs to be done, shopping, cook-ing, and cleaning. And let's not talk about the weekend entertainment that we must provide for our families in order to keep the peace and our own sanity. Oh yeah, I get it. But, somehow, you have to find a way to put your passion into service.

One of my favorite places on the Internet to read about what great causes people are donating their time to is www.idealist.org They post thousands of volunteer opportunities right on their Web site. You can make a long term commitment to a cause, or you can just sign up for one day projects that will make a difference in the lives of the people of your community. You may even be able to start a group that will be interested in supporting a cause that's near and dear to your heart. There are tons of possibilities; seek and you will be sure to find. One great organization is www.malecare.org , the nonprofit that I and the Black Dad Connection is part of.

58. BE MORE—Nowadays dads must provide more than just financial stability, but you already knew that.

There was a time when a man was considered the sole provider for his family, and pretty much nothing more. He went off into the woods, mountains, plains, fields, and lakes, and he clubbed, stabbed, or beat the crap out of some beast with his fists and brought it home to his woman and his kids. He would grunt proudly, his family would swoon in awe of his bravery and strength—it was all good. If the urge took hold of him, after he devoured the flesh of his kill, he would drag his woman by the bone in her hair to some quiet place behind a rock, where he would yet again prove his manhood.

Nowadays our mountains and plains have been replaced by supermarkets, our clubs and fists by college degrees. Those of us with adventurous spirits can still get a little nookie behind a rock, but my guess is that we are mostly doing our man thing on beds. Instead of grunting we, um…OK we still grunt, however, we also talk and communicate in a bunch of new ways (belching = "good dinner, Honey," nose picking = "please pass me a tissue"). With all of these changes, it's no longer enough for us to bring home a paycheck and pay the cost of living. In fact many of us probably need our wives or partners to bring home a paycheck if we want to make our mortgage payment. The time of the "breadwinner" has come and gone. The playing field has been leveled, at least as far as domestic relationships go, and that changes the game.

With the rules of the family constantly being revised, the one thing that remains consistent is the idea of teamwork. Teamwork, simply put, is two or more people working together towards a common goal. As a member of any team you are required to play your role and carry your fair share of the load. So as a father, you are expected to do your part and that no longer means bringing home a paycheck and kissing the kids goodnight We have to nurture the kids, read to the kids, play with the kids, and take them to interesting places. We have to wash the dishes, occasionally cook (only the things that you like to cook or are good at cooking), and pitch in with the cleaning. And don't forget one of the best parts of this partnership crap: the other has to do her share and get her booty on top. So there are benefits.

59. BE A DREAMER—You have to dream big dreams in this life for the sake of you and your family.

I am a dreamer. I once lived off of the images that were fed to me by cable television and lifestyle magazines. Then I moved into an apartment that did not allow cable or satellite television and I got a hold of myself. I started to realize that I lived in a real world, not one constructed for me by MTV. For some people, seeing the rich and famous in all of their fabulousness can be a motivational force that would otherwise be non-existent in their lives. For others it is a detriment and feeds bitterness and envy, and often can lead to a mental paralysis where all you can think about is what you don't have. Sometimes this kind of thinking breeds irrational and reckless behavior that eventually can give birth to a person willing to do anything for money and anything to be able to fake the wealthy life. What would you do for fame and money?

Like I said, I fantasize about private jets, Mercedes Benzes, dining with movie stars and countless other things (there's just something about Cristina Millian). But I don't let the fantasies get in the way of my reality, because my reality is pretty great most of the time.

It's perfectly OK to dream, so long as you keep steady footing in the real world. In the real world, bills need to be paid on time to protect your credit rating. Responsibilities need to be tended to and followed-through with whether they are to your family, work or any of your other priorities. We would all like to be able to quit a job we hate and then have our dream job handed to us by a mysterious stranger, the job fairy if you will. But that doesn't happen very often. It happens; I'll concede that, we've heard the stories of how great talents have been discovered. It has just never happened to me.

When my son was born, I was fifteen credits shy of graduating, and fifteen minutes from losing my mind. At the time I was earning $27,000 a year as an office manager at a mental health clinic, and my wife was on leave from her social work job at a hospital. Luckily, through the generosity of our co-workers and a few family members, we were well-stocked with baby stuff and ready to go. And due to a lot of early planning and preparation (we knew she was pregnant at two weeks), including the renewal of a college loan, cutting back on therapy, and quickly filing tax returns, we were able to pay many of our largest bills six months in advance and were able to focus my income on rent and utilities and food. A nice little cushion in terms of time, yes, but not comfortable by any means. If a single emergency of any kind had occurred (flat tire, dead batteries in the TV remote control) we would have been screwed. So I started dreaming.

I wanted to start a publishing company, sell houses, start a non-profit, write a fiction novel, start a magazine, buy stocks (with magic beans perhaps), sell crack, sell blood, sell sex, get a second job, start a record label, write a screenplay, get into eBay, you name it. But in the end, I decided to focus my energies on finishing school and reading every "how-to" book I could find on the subjects I just mentioned. I had gotten too close to finishing college to quit, and I had no seed money to get anything else off the ground, which made the decision rather simple to me.

Yet somehow poor people always end up scrounging up just enough dough to put together a craptastic rap demo that no one will listen to, when the money could have gone into the stock market or any of thousands of better "investments" that may have netted enough money to put a down payment on a recording studio. A friend of mine from high school and college worked full time, went to school full time, and by having a decent job was able to build a respectable multithousand dollar recording studio in his parent's basement piece by piece. Plus he had his own apartment several miles away. He taught himself how to use the equipment because in college he learned how to take a systematic approach to figuring shit out. Essentially, in college he learned how to learn. This seems to be paying off being that several people in the business have expressed an interest in working with him and up and coming artist are paying him for recording studio time.

A good way to go about chasing your dreams is by taking the part-time approach. Do all the things you need to do to survive for right now, which is get a job and go to college and get a degree if you haven't done so already. Don't be one of the many that has nothing to fall back on once the dream officially becomes deferred. I secured my first post-bachelors job three months after graduation and it was $10K more than what I was making prior to my being able to put my degree on my resume. This is a significant raise in the non-profit world, where I labor away for the greater good almost every day. With that job, I was able to purchase equipment for one of my side ventures and a laptop computer for my writing. Without it I would not have the tools I needed for creative output. I still actively chase my dreams and by putting this book out, I'm living one right now.

EPILOGUE

<u>GO TO COLLEGE</u>—This is the last of my advice and musings. Share it with someone who needs it. College has definitely made me a better dad, though I'll be the first to say that you can be amazing without a degree.

College. I remember it with great fondness. The drunken frat parties where I often out-guzzled the most devoted beer-guzzling stooges. The long nights slipped into the dawn as we listened to Bob Marley while smoking the best darn ganja in town and indulging in "deep" conversation. We would spend hours philosophizing about the sudden emergence of the "white girl with a fat booty." My theories on that subject usually centered around clothing designers getting slick with jean cuts, while my associates would argue about evolution requiring them to develop ass in order to compete with the J-Los and Beyoncé's of the world. To this day I refused to believe it was that deep; it simply has to be the jeans.

When not reaping the nutritional benefits of barley and hops, or debating new evolutionary hypotheses enshrouded in a relaxed herbal haze, I was spending my time having sex. Tons of sex. Unadulterated monkey sex. The girls were so plentiful and varied in college that I can honestly say that I never had to taste the same flavor twice. Why would I? That would be like going to

Baskin Robbins and always ordering one scoop of vanilla. It's like having cable and only watching PBS. I refused to forgo variety for stability. And I made it a point to never remember the name of a girl I planned to do nasty things to. I wanted to focus my mind on sexual creativity, and stuffing a name in my brain that I would only use once or twice made no sense. I was depleting my stock of brain cells as it was. I had many conversations that went something like this:

"Hey…you." I'd say. I always remember a face.

"Hi Keith, I had a really great time last night."

"Glad to hear it, beautiful." They liked that name. It made them feel, well, beautiful.

"Maybe you can call me later," she'd say. I would be thinking *not a chance ugly*.

"Sure, babe."

And that'd be it. If I saw her again I'd act all sad and depressed and stressed about school. Most girls have no tolerance for a sappy, weepy, punk-of-a-man and will likely avoid you after a well-played breakdown. I can honestly say that every man should go to college for the girls. There tend to be so many of them and so few of us black guys that we can most often have our way with just about anybody. I once had a line outside my door and ladies were taking numbers and making appointments. College is a sexual free-for-all and I gave it away, free, for all. And I can't even talk about the spring breaks in Cancun.

Not Superdad

And if you believe that crap, I'd also like to tell you about a bridge in Brooklyn that my real estate company just put on the market.

For me, college was a place to get a degree that would in turn make me a more attractive candidate for employers. I have known too many people in my young life that flunked out of college, not because they are un-intelligent, but because they could not find the balance between school and socializing that one must have to be truly successful in school. I am actually in favor of tipping the scales in favor of school and forgetting about balancing anything. I avoided making friends as much as possible. In part because I also worked full time, but also because I felt like I had become an adult and need-ed to set aside the HS mentality that too many people bring with them to higher education.

There was no reason, in my mind, to make new friends. I had my old friends from junior high and a couple of buddies I had picked up along the way and that was more than sufficient. It wasn't until I met my future wife (at work) two years into my college educa-tion that I began to think about life beyond the two places where I spent most of my time. And the only rea-son that I thought it would work with her was because she had completed college already while working full time so she could relate to what I was trying to accom-plish and did not try to monopolize my time. Don't get me wrong, I enjoy a good time, but for the four or five years of school that you are paying for it is important to prioritize.

Keith Devin Morton

I took about 18 months off between high school and higher education to work because I had no plan, which was unfortunate. I graduated from a great specialized high school in Brooklyn where I had to pass an exam to get in. But what happened was that the sheer size of the school forced many kids with great potential, including myself, to be an afterthought when it came to preparing for college. The guidance counselors meant well, but they were spread thin over the 1100 student graduating class. They tended to give those with average GPAs a quick once over and focused their energy on those that were in the top 10%. Under the circumstances I understand the logic; however it did nothing for me. I had a less-than-solid C+ average (79%), but in the grand scheme that was good for that school.

Neither of my parents graduated from college and at the time I had two older brothers that had their own school woes to concern themselves with. I was on my own. No one asked me if I planned on going to school, it was a foregone conclusion that eventually I would and it was left at that. Everyone supported the idea; they just couldn't help me with the details of selecting a school, filling out applications, setting up tours, etc. It would have been much easier if one of my parents had an Alma Mater that they donated to that I could fall back on.

I had a supervisor at a job that I loved who encouraged me to pursue a degree. That encouragement may have changed my life. Sometimes there is an inexplicable pull from within that directs you to your destiny. It's often not blatant, but rather a gentle tugging, that if you're not careful you may mistake for gas.

Frustrated and poor, I knew that my best option would be public education. Of course, I would have relished the opportunity to attend an Ivy League school like my eldest brother, but my grades and funding would not allow for that dream at that moment. If nothing else I understood the importance of setting realistic goals. So, a year after graduating high school, I called the City University of New York and requested an application. They waived the application fee because I was able to prove that I was on some kind of public assistance at the time (did I mention I was poor?). A week or so later the application arrived and much to my chagrin it looked like gibberish to me.

I did not realize that there were so many schools that specialized in so many things! I hadn't thought much about what I wanted to study in school; I just knew I wanted to go. Did I want to focus on business? Writing? Liberal Arts? The sciences? I had no clue. I knew, after four years of High School studying Civil Engineering that I did not want to be an engineer. A friend of mine up the street went to Hunter College and she was graduating soon with plans to go to law school. That sounded like a plan to me. I selected Hunter as my first choice, Baruch second, Brooklyn third and so on. I made some copies of my application and off it went. I had finally taken the first step toward attaining a degree and fulfilling some of my pent up potential. It felt good.

Then the acceptance letter came, and I almost cried like a little girl. Had I started the water works, they would not have been tears of joy. CUNY, not knowing me from a hole in a wall, had done their calculations and decided that my GPA sucked gorilla nuts and offered me a community college. Not just any community college (I don't have anything against community college, I just had not considered it as an option) but one that was about two hours away by bus. My college hopes and dreams had been crushed, just like that. I would never be able to keep my job and travel to and from a school in what I considered the middle of nowhere. Sure it was in Brooklyn, but a part I was far from. Somewhere on the letter it mentioned the location where a disgruntled applicant could go to discuss other options. Damn right I wanted to discuss my options. At the very least I had to know why I was accepted to a school that wasn't even on my list. In what I thought must be a positive sign from the heavens, I discovered that the office where I would have to go to talk to a college counselor was literally next door to where I was working at the time. I could stop by on my lunch break.

When I stepped into the CUNY office clutching the notification letter in a sweaty hand I knew that it was going to be a long lunch break. People of every race and nationality populated the room and wore their hopes and dreams on their faces like tribal masks. It was a tribe of knowledge seekers looking toward a future of employment and respect. I took a number and was engulfed by a feeling of organized chaos as my eyes scanned the room looking for a seat. Some of the prospective students speaking with their counselors were clearly getting bad news: they were visibly shaken and emotional. Others acted as if they had just won a pageant of some kind. They smiled and waved at whoever made eye contact with them. There was pacing and quiet whispering, eagerness and resignation. I was impressed to see the number of parents that were in the waiting area with their young offspring. Moms and dads that were determined to ensure that their kids received the educations they themselves never did. Most of the parents were there for moral support. It must have been like having your own personal cheering squad shaking their invisible pompoms, never taking notice of the score.

When my number was called, I steadied myself to state my case.

"Hi. I got this letter in the mail the other day and I'm not sure I understand it. I don't even know where this school is." The counselor then told me where it was and how to get there. "I can't do that. I work up the block. Do I have any other options?" She told me my other option. In my head it wasn't an option. "I can't believe this. I went to one of the best high schools in the city and I can't get into Hunter? This is insane. Is there anyone else I can talk to? Anything else I can do?"

Then she asked the $100,000 question: "Did you take the SATs?" Of course I took the SATs. I had no choice in the matter as I recall it. I told her my score and then she informed me that if I could provide her with proof of my score I could go to the four- year college of my choice.

Good news like that was infrequent, especially when you lived in a neighborhood like Bedford Stuyvesant, where good news was often limited to the declaration that you made it safely from the subway to your home.

Needless to say my workday couldn't end fast enough. I sat at the front desk of the mental health clinic where my career in non-profit began with answering phones. I performed my receptionist duties on autopilot while going over in my head all of the places where I could have put the copies of my scores. At 8 o'clock I raced home, my feet and the train both moving too slow for my taste, and dug my scores out of the bottom of the box I had stuffed them in after considering them worthless garbage. My sleep that night was filled with sweet anxiety like that of a person who just won the lottery.

The next day I went to the CUNY office on my lunch break and handed in my scores. The counselor working on my case made copies, inputted the numbers into her terminal, made a few changes then pres-to—I was going to my first choice college.

"You'll get an acceptance letter from Hunter in a week or two. Good luck," she said. And that was that. I was going to college with the confidence that comes with fighting for your place and proving your case.

I have said this many times and to many people: College is an exercise in patience. If you are an instant-gratification kind of person, you will have to adjust your thinking when you commit yourself to college. A semester is what it is, and that's nearly five months of your life and usually 12 to 15 credits toward a 120 credit degree. Some of the students, the ones that I could not relate to, were taking 18 or 21 credits because they lived with their parents and did not have jobs. I had no such luxuries. I'll admit that I was, and in some ways still am, a straight up hater when it comes to people with even the tiniest bit of privilege as it relates to college. Those people that waltz out of college without the burden of thousands of dollars in debt. I would have graduated in three years instead of five had I been taken care of by my Mommy and Daddy. I may have even then had the urge to get a Master's degree in something right after earning the BA. But, alas, I was destined to fill out financial aid applications, loan applications, book vouchers, and everything else.

Halfway through my education, it was determined by some higher power that my $20K/year job was more than enough to pay for school, feed myself, and pay rent and bills. My aid was cut and I was forced to take out a loan, which as of this writing I am still paying back. That being said I also make much more money than what I was making just prior to graduation, which obviously makes it worth every penny.

Here's What I Really Learned:

1. You don't have to be a genius to be in college, just dedicated, patient, and kind of focused.
I realized early on that colleges are businesses and they have a vested interest in every student's suc-

cess. They can't boast that they have the highest rate of job placement after graduation if the students aren't graduating. Colleges want you to graduate—and then come back for a Master's degree so you can graduate again. They also want you to be employable so that you can one day become a generous donor that they can name something after. Your failure goes into their statistics and they don't want that. That's why most, if not all, university systems offer tutoring, language labs, computer access, extended library hours, psychiatric counseling, writing workshops, and anything else they can think of to foster your success. No one is going to force you to use all these tools that they offer though. You have to be honest with yourself and know what academic areas you are deficient in. Learn that early on and use the resources wisely.

2. Choose a major you like.

When it's time to choose a major, pick something that you like and won't be frustrated with after the first semester. Hating your major often leads to dropping out. If you truly despise chemistry, don't be a chem. major. Especially if your only rationale is the serious salary. You don't want to risk failure because you are chasing a high-paying job path that may or may not work out. Failure is the breeding ground for discouragement, and discouragement will almost certainly lead to dropping out. You don't want to wind up paying for a degree that you never actually received. After talking to a counselor and professors in the department, I chose Urban Studies for my major. It was a small major, which I liked, that studied urban planning and social issues. It also had strong research and analysis components; two things that scared the crap out of me, even though I enjoyed them both. It was the major for me. We talked at length about issues and theories that I was passionate about, in classes that restricted enrollment to the students in my major, which made life in school much more tolerable.

3. Read the assignments.

This may seem obvious, but it's not. By cramming you may be able to stuff enough information into your short term memory to help you pass a multiple choice exam, but it is a terrible technique when it comes to essay exams. One of my most memorable moments in college was in an African Studies class called *Intro to Black Politics*. In that class I participated regularly and added insight to the discussion that can only come from someone born in Key West and raised in Bed-Stuy. I adored the class and had a great deal of respect for the professor and the way that he taught his class with such intensity that bordered on psychosis.

He did not fear retribution from the white students that were often left aghast and disturbed by his discourse. Biting his tongue and compromising his own personal values was not on his to-do list. Students would run off like punks and complain to the department head and others in power about how he seemed "racist." It did not deter him one bit. I was proud of him for sticking to his guns even when others would have cowered. Then one day I got my first essay exam in his class back. I had failed. It was the first test I had failed in college. After picking my jaw off from the ground I visited my favorite-turned-most despised professor during his office hours. He was one of the few college instructors that I had known to have a line outside his office. Several students visited him to shoot the breeze and talk about black political thought. Not me. I went there to talk business.

"I studied for this test, Professor. If I failed, then obviously it was way too hard for an intro class. You know I know this stuff," I told him

"You do, but it wasn't reflected in the exam, brother."

"Yeah, because the way you asked the questions was too hard and confusing"

"Did you read the assignments?"

"Of course." I had read most of them anyway.

"Then you should have done better." He sat back in his chair and continued. "Why are you really here? What do you want to talk about?"

"What's up with this grade? Why did you fail me?" I asked. My ego was more hurt than anything and I started to wonder if I was intelligent.

"I didn't fail you, brother. You failed yourself. There were white people in this class that got A's on the same exam. I have students just like you every year that come into my class and think that because they are black they have all the answers and they know the material. Then they come and sit in that same chair and say exactly what you just said to me. Brother, just because you have lived racism doesn't mean you can pass my exams.

Next time you should study harder and you will do well. Is there anything else?"

There was nothing I could say to that. In my heart, I knew he was right. That lesson will stick with me for as long as I live. But not just the part about studying harder—also, the message that experience is a great educator, but that knowledge is in the written word.

4. Take an African or Black Studies class (or a few).

From elementary through high school you only get 50% of the story on just about everything, except maybe Black history, where you get about 3%. Our teachers in the early years of our education glossed over Martin Luther King Jr. and make him into kind of the teddy bear of social change. He is taken out of context and his words twisted to make every other point besides the ones he was actually trying to make. We are often led to believe that black history began with the advent of race-based slavery, which is a shameful and destructive untruth. We may get a snippet on Bessie Coleman or Madame CJ Walker or Langston Hughes, but those names, as great as they are, do not scratch the surface of black history. Then along came college where I took Black Politics and the History of Haiti among others and learned more about black history in those classes than I had in my entire life. I started thinking about the colonization of Africa, and its impact on contemporary politics, something I had never done before. I gained an intimate knowledge of the Haitian Revolution and how Toussaint l'Overture, the leader of the revolution, repelled an invasion by Napoleon Bonaparte. I learned that Black people had religion, culture, governments, and kingdoms, all before the European influence.

Black history has many myths, legends, and explorers and adventurers, inventions and technological advances. All that life-changing information inspired me and it helped earn me a college degree. Those classes were worth three credits just like all the others! African Studies classes are a win/win for black people and also of value to our white counterparts. They too, should know, and are entitled to, the full scope of history.

5. *Use the library.*

Of course you can act "deep" and read about your history in the Library, but you can also take a nice nap there as well. What I am about to say is just plain wrong that's why I felt compelled to acknowledge it before I say it: I got some of my best sleep in between classes at the library. When I had spent the evening before poring over a textbook in preparation for an exam or discussion, it was a welcome break to sit in the dim, quiet library, and take a few minutes to recharge. After my son was born it was a home away from home and its chairs were my beds. I had the best spots staked out in the deepest, darkest, most private places the library had to offer.

It was also a decent place to study, especially right before an exam. Quiet is a necessity when it comes to deep concentration and any library that's worth its salt is nothing if it isn't quiet. I know a bunch of people (whom I would love to smack) that insist they cannot function if they are not in a noisy place. "I like to study in the hall with the people passing by talking. It helps me concentrate." Or, "I have to have the TV on if I want to get any work done." I can't believe that people can say these things with a straight face. All I had to do was smuggle some highly caffeinated coffee into the library. That's where I got the good studying done—on the days when I wasn't napping, of course.

6. Keep holding on

There were several good reasons for me to have dropped out of school. I was going into debt, I had a son on the way, I was seeing a life coach regularly, I wasn't getting much sleep, I had a demanding job in non-profit, and so on. I would come home after midnight some evenings then wake up at five to do it again. People close to me were dropping out of school left and right for financial and academic reasons, and to fulfill family obligations. I knew my family and friends would understand if I took some time off. But I couldn't bring myself to take a break. I don't know why, but I couldn't. My wife (who was my girlfriend for the early years I was in school) would remind me of the fact that I was almost done (she said that for three years straight; I guess she kind of hustled me). If you take a look at my college transcripts you can chart the years that I was having tough times in my personal life as well as where I was enjoying success, but what you will not see is a break. Like Nas said many years ago "I never sleep because sleep is the cousin of death."

Some days were tougher than others. On occasion the words wouldn't flow for a research paper, or a concept taught in a lecture wouldn't stick, or a reading assignment was too long for me to get any other work done for other classes. In those instances, I would have to sacrifice a good score on an exam that was a low percentage of the grade to focus on a larger assignment in another class. Another strategy was to figure out what the lowest possible grade was that I could get on a final exam in order to pass a class and work toward that goal. Nine out of ten times my goal was to pass a class, and if the A came I'd be happy. More often than not, the A did come and my stress and calculating paid off.

I would also visit the professors during their office hours. One of my greatest lessons in college was that if you are on the edge of failing a class and you visited the professor to discuss your concerns, you'd have a much better chance of passing. It worked almost the same way if you were on the edge of an A. It's true that some professors will fail you or give you the B no matter what you do or how charming you think you are, but their remembering your name and face can never hurt. Understanding the system and a professor's style was essential to being successful throughout college.

By the way, with a full time job managing staff *and* a clinic, in addition to a wife and a child for my last year in school, I was able to graduate with honors (*Cum Laude*) in five years. If I can, anyone can.

AFTERWORD

On an unseasonably cold night in early spring, sitting in TGI Friday's eating shrimp and chicken fingers with the family—about two years after the bulk of this book was written—I told my son that I wrote a book about him and me being his dad. I decided to tell him this because I had read the book the night before in its current form and realized that he is the "star." I was somewhat startled by the revelation and felt it only right to mention it to my almost-six-year-old. I wondered if when he was old enough to really sit down and read the book (he can do it now but I don't think he'd take much from it) if he'd be upset at me for writing it or if he'd see it for what it is: an earnest effort to help black fathers, and any other fathers who may be able to relate. Consequently the wife and I explained to him as best way we could the goals of the book and asked if he'd be ok with taking a pivotal role in helping some of the daddies who read the book become better fathers. He thought about it longer than I would have liked. Thankfully he finally gave us the thumbs up. Had he put up the longest finger on his hand instead of the thumb we would have had a problem.

With Dev's approval still fresh I started to think about the best way to close out the book. A difficult task when you think about putting a period (or better yet and exclamation point!) on a section of your life that changed you forever. Just thinking about making such an effort seemed to hover in the realm of the impossible. Part of me feels that this book lays bare, and for the world to see and critique, a chunk of my family's life that is personal and not necessarily for general consumption. Yet this other part of me, the part that kept me at the computer, is the one that understands the value of sharing such intimate moments. I'm not a reality TV star, and neither is my son. I'm just convinced that this story was meant to be told and that someone, somewhere will find it helpful. Someone will be able to feel that they are not washed up alone on the deserted island of fatherhood—I'm washed up right next to you…and I brought beer. We're together in this on some weird metaphysical level even if we never meet.

When President Obama called us, black fathers, out during his campaign at first I was defiant and thinking "I've been a good dad from day one, he ain't talkin' to me!" But of course he was. I have yet to ascend to the ranks of *great* father and as far as I'm concerned that designation will not be mine to claim until my son has graduated from college and started to do his part to make a way for those on his heels to follow his lead. Then I will say I have achieved greatness in this fatherhood thing. I have a long way to go before I get there and I know that. The wife and I survived the terrible twos through fours and it was a fantastic accomplishment. But this isn't the time to start throwing parties and congratulating each other on a job well done. There is no time for victory dances in the end zone. Adolescence is only a few short years away. Now is the time to get back into the huddle and prepare for the next play. The boy hasn't even taken his first standardized test yet!

Still, my biggest accomplishment since the birth of my son has been building a connection to him as his daddy—one that will be hard to break. We have spent quality time together and have shared laughs that will help us to forge ahead in our relationship with the best chance possible of surviving any daddy/son drama. We have laid a foundation of reinforced steel and man-rock that will not be easily broken. Many dads do not have this kind of chance because they are not with the mother of their child, or they simply lack the confidence needed to be a present and connected dad. To them I say hang in there, it is not too late, you just have to do some catching up and perhaps take the initiative in a way that not even you knew you could. It's never too late to be a major player in your child's life—you mainly have to have a desire that overwhelmingly motivates you to do so. With that desire you will find a way to get past the hurdles in your way, I promise you.

I'm not going to rattle off statistics to you, dear reader, about how dire the current fatherhood situation is in black America. It's unnecessary in the grand scheme. Unnecessary because we know darn well that it's bad because it's been bad for some time now. It is grossly irrelevant what percentage of the black children live without a daddy in the home because we live next door to these families and we see the children, we know the faces and results of father absenteeism in our communities. We know it because we live it. We also know the results of lousy fathers sticking around to the detriment of the family. We know what harm some *present* fathers pose, the men who could care less about their offspring, men who are not fit to own a dog much less be a parent. And we also know the fathers who give it their all and still struggle to be successful because they are building up a child without a manual, and often without being able to reach out to their own fathers for advice because he's been long gone. We know the great dads who amaze us and inspire us with their love and strength. We know them all because we are them.

Certainly we are moving in the right direction towards being better parents and trying to leave the past in the past when it comes to so-called "daddy issues" that many of us cling to for no reason other than believing wholeheartedly that we have to blame somebody. Obama challenged us to do better and implored us to step up our game for the sake of our families. He reminded us that financially supporting a child does not make you a father; it makes you an ATM. Being present, dynamic, and active is what makes you a father. And sometimes that means giving up a televised baseball games, or putting down the remote and going to the park. It may mean suffering through a long drawn out tea party with invisible tea and stuffed toys as guests. But the long term effects of that kind of interaction is insanely positive and is usually more fun than it seems when you are asked to do it. What's more, I have discovered is that even something as innocuous as teatime may make you a better human being, not just father.

This Is It, Really

When it's all said and done, when the long crazy days are over and I'm lying next to my wife at night listening to her breathe, I think about my life and my personal growth. I try not to dwell on the negative and wonder if my heart is in the right place as I tackle my little section of the black fatherhood issue while a world of problems face us. I think about the patience that I have developed because fatherhood forced me to step outside of myself and be better. I think about the listener that I have become, and how every aspect of my life including my marriage and my career have benefited from my being a better listener. With children you often have to listen with your instincts and your heart, not just your ears, and that idea transfers well to every other aspect of your life. I also think about how money has become much less of a driving force in my life because my family has survived, even flourished, with very little help from dead presidents.

I am not a perfect dad. I see no reason to perpetuate such an image, an untrue image. In my opinion there is too much of that kind of phoniness permeating the media and the national consciousness. However, that does not mean that I, or any other father, am allowed to aim only as high as mid-level mediocrity. It simply means that I have accepted that I am a human being and as such, even in fatherhood, I will have moments of reflection where I will say to myself *I could have handled a particular situation better.* In those instances I will learn whatever lesson there is, and move on. No sense in kicking myself and getting stuck. I predict that there are many things that I will not get right, but it will not be because of a lack of effort. It will be because even at its best, life is imperfect and everything will not always go as planned. I am proud to say that thus far the things I have got right have far outweighed the areas where I have missed a step or two. The wheels of this life, and of my time on this earth as a father are in motion and I intend on using the momentum that I built in the early years to propel me to the finish line. At least that's the plan. As I imagine the future I keep telling myself that co-parenting a child during the tween years and then head first into puberty will be fun, the same way cliff diving into alligator infested waters could be fun. Cowabunga.